The
Apple Watch Series 10
User Guide For Seniors

Tips and Tricks for Maximizing Performance, Productivity, and Mastering Your Device

Ray V. Lopez

Contents

Introduction

Welcome to the World of Apple Watch Series 10

Did you know that over 100 million people around the world wear an Apple Watch every day? And here's something even more interesting—an increasing proportion of these users are seniors, just like you. Indeed. More and more older folks are embracing technology, and the Apple Watch Series 10 is becoming a trusted friend for staying connected, staying active, and staying secure.

The Apple Watch Series 10 is not just a watch. It's a tool designed to make your life easier, healthier, and more pleasurable. It's like having a small but powerful assistant right on your wrist, ready to help you with everyday activities, keep track of your health, and even provide peace of mind in case of crises.

You might be wondering: Is this really for me? Maybe you've never owned a smartwatch before, or maybe you've struggled with technology in the past. The good news is, you don't need to be a tech guru to enjoy what the Apple Watch has to offer.

Whether you want to monitor your heart rate, get reminders to take a walk, or just know who's calling without having to dig through your bag or pockets, this device can make a major impact in your daily life.

Technology nowadays is evolving rapidly, but that doesn't mean you have to be left behind. In fact, the Apple Watch Series 10 was created with simplicity and accessibility in mind, making it one of the most senior-friendly wearables on the market. It's time to investigate what this powerful small device can accomplish for you.

Why This Guide Is Perfect for Seniors

Now, you may have seen other instructions or manuals before—some crammed with technical language, tiny type, or perplexing illustrations. That's not what you'll find here.

This handbook was specifically built for seniors, with your requirements, your speed, and your lifestyle in mind. We recognize that learning something new can be tough at times, especially when it comes to technology. But with the correct approach, it doesn't have to be frustrating. In fact, it may be joyful, powerful, and even fun.

Here's why this guide is different from others:

1. Clear, Easy-to-Follow Instructions

Every function, every process, is explained in basic, straightforward terms. There's no rushing, no pressure. We walk through each component of the Apple Watch Series 10 slowly and methodically, so you feel confident at every level.

2. Focus on What Matters Most to You

This book focuses on the elements that seniors care about the most—health monitoring, emergency safety tools, maintaining in touch with loved ones, and making daily living simpler. You won't be weighed down with features you'll never use.

3. Tips and Tricks Tailored for Seniors

You'll uncover valuable suggestions based on real-life use, specifically for elders. Whether it's altering the text size to make things easier to read, or setting up reminders for medicine, we've got you covered.

4. Confidence-Boosting

Many seniors have told us they feel uncomfortable about utilizing new technology. This guide is here to change that. We want you to feel empowered, independent, and in control of your device.

Whether you are 60, 70, or even 80+ years young, this approach respects your experience and appreciates your courage to try something new. It's never too late to learn, and the results can be truly life-enhancing.

How to Use This Book

Let's speak about how this book works. You don't need to read it from start to end in one sitting (unless you want to!). Think of it as a pleasant companion—something you can turn to whenever you have a question or want to learn something new.

Here's how you can get the most out of this guide:

Start with the Basics

If you're entirely new to the Apple Watch, begin with the first few chapters. These cover the essentials: unboxing, charging, and setting up your watch. These sections will help you become comfortable with your device in a relaxed and easy way.

Learn at Your Own Pace

You are in control. Read a bit each day, or spend time perfecting one feature before moving on to the next. There's no deadline, no test at the end—just helpful knowledge created for you.

Refer Back Anytime

Can't remember how to adjust the brightness or check your step count? No issue. This guide is organized in a way that makes it easy to flip back and get what you need quickly.

Explore What Interests You

Maybe you're thrilled about the health features, or maybe you want to utilize your watch to remain in touch with your family. Skip to the chapters that interest you most. You can always come back to other parts later.

Keep It Handy

Your Apple Watch will become part of your daily routine, and so can this book. Keep it at your side as you explore, and it will act as a continual source of support and encouragement.

Key Features of the Apple Watch Series 10

The Apple Watch Series 10 is not just another smartwatch—it's an innovative tool meant to integrate seamlessly into your lifestyle, whether you're trying to improve your health, stay connected, or simply make your daily routine easier. If you're new to the world of smartwatches or haven't yet explored everything the Series 10 has to offer, this tutorial is your first step toward understanding this sophisticated device. The Apple Watch Series 10 comes equipped with a range of capabilities that are not just new but geared to fit the demands of every user, even seniors.

1. Sleek and Comfortable Design

First and foremost, the Apple Watch Series 10 is designed with comfort in mind. It's lightweight and can be worn all day without pain, which is vital when you want a device that's always on your wrist. The Series 10 is also water-resistant, so you don't have to worry about taking it off when washing your hands or even swimming.

The display is composed of sapphire crystal, which is durable and resistant to scratches, ensuring the watch stays looking new for longer. Its exquisite design makes it not simply useful, but also fashionable. With changeable bands available, you can choose the one that best fits your own style.

2. Advanced Health Monitoring Features

One of the major features of the Apple Watch Series 10 is its ability to help you track your health and well-being in real-time. This is particularly critical for elderly who may need to track their vital signs more routinely. The Series 10 contains various health sensors that make it easy to stay on top of your wellness:

- **Heart Rate Monitoring**: The Apple Watch can measure your heart rate throughout the day, alerting you if it detects any irregularities. It's a simple way to keep an eye on your heart health without needing a visit to the doctor.

- **ECG (Electrocardiogram)**: With the Series 10, you can take an ECG anytime, anywhere. This feature helps detect irregular heart rhythms, such as atrial fibrillation (AFib), which is crucial for early detection and treatment.

- **Blood Oxygen Monitoring**: Another advanced feature is the ability to measure your blood oxygen levels. Low levels of oxygen can be a sign of serious health conditions, and the Apple Watch makes it easy to check and stay informed.

- **Fall Detection**: If you fall while wearing the watch, it can detect the fall and alert emergency contacts. If you're unable to respond, the watch will automatically call emergency services, giving you peace of mind knowing help is only a button press away.

3. Activity and Fitness Tracking

Staying active is vital for maintaining good health at any age, and the Apple Watch Series 10 makes it easier than ever to track your activity. With built-in activity rings, the watch gives visual feedback to encourage you to keep active throughout the day. The rings reflect your Move, Exercise, and Stand goals, providing you a clear image of how much you're moving.

The watch automatically records your steps, calories burned, and even distance traveled, while also delivering customized training recommendations. Whether you're walking, running, cycling, or doing yoga, the Apple Watch Series 10 monitors your progress and gives you feedback on how you may improve.

4. Emergency Features

Your safety is a primary focus with the Apple Watch Series 10. In addition to the fall detection functionality stated earlier, the Series 10 contains an SOS Emergency function, which allows you to call emergency services with a simple touch of a button. Whether you're dealing with a medical emergency or need assistance in a dangerous situation, the Apple Watch Series 10 ensures aid is always at hand.

5. Connectivity

The Apple Watch Series 10 helps you stay connected to what matters most. It can sync with your iPhone, so you can receive calls, texts, and notifications right on your watch. This is especially handy for elderly who may have difficulties reaching for their phone when it rings.

If you have a cellular form of the Apple Watch, you can even make calls, send texts, and browse the internet without needing your iPhone nearby. This degree of connectivity is great for remaining in touch with family members, caretakers, or friends at all times.

What's New in watchOS 11

watchOS 11, the operating system that runs the Apple Watch Series 10, comes with several exciting new features and updates meant to improve both use and performance. Whether you're an experienced Apple Watch user or a novice, watchOS 11 provides major enhancements that will make your experience smoother and more efficient.

1. Enhanced Health Tracking

One of the greatest additions in watchOS 11 is the Health app. It now provides more thorough and precise health statistics than ever before, including greater interaction with your iPhone's health data. This means you can track your workout progress and health information in one convenient area.

Additionally, the Sleep Tracking tool has been updated, giving you a more detailed overview of your sleep quality and helping you create better sleep habits. Seniors might especially benefit from this, as good quality sleep is vital for general health.

2. New Watch Faces

Customization is one of the attractions of watchOS 11. The upgrade provides new watch faces that are not only gorgeous but also more practical. You may now choose from a range of complications (tiny widgets that offer brief information) to personalize your watch face. Whether you want to view the weather, your heart rate, or the next event on your calendar, you can have it all on your watch face at a glance.

3. Smarter Siri Integration

Siri, Apple's voice assistant, has also received some substantial changes in watchOS 11. It's now smarter, faster, and more intuitive, making it easier for you to ask questions, create reminders, or control your smart home devices. Siri can even let you write messages, start exercises, or obtain directions—all without needing to lift a finger.

4. More Seamless Connectivity with iPhone

watchOS 11 enhances the way your Apple Watch connects to your iPhone. It provides better syncing for texts, notifications, and apps. The updates also enhance battery economy, allowing your Apple Watch to run longer throughout the day, even with heavy usage.

5. Streamlined Notifications and Alerts

watchOS 11 makes it easier than ever to handle your notifications. Now, you can filter and prioritize notifications so that you only receive alerts that matter most. Whether you're getting updates from your fitness tracker or reminders from your calendar, watchOS 11 ensures they're structured and easy to follow.

Frequently Asked Questions from Seniors

As with any new gadget, it's reasonable to have a few questions, especially when it comes to something as complex as the Apple Watch Series 10. Below, we've compiled some of the most common questions we get from seniors, along with their solutions, to assist soothe any concerns you may have.

1. How do I set up my Apple Watch for the first time?

Setting up your Apple Watch is basic. The watch pairs with your iPhone via Bluetooth, and once connected, the Apple Watch app will walk you through the setup procedure. You'll be requested to adjust settings including language, display choices, and health preferences. If you need help, the step-by-step directions in this guide will walk you through each element of the setup.

2. Is the Apple Watch Series 10 difficult to use?

Not at all! The Apple Watch Series 10 is designed with simplicity in mind. The UI is easy, and the watch contains helpful features like voice commands and visual tips to assist with activities. Additionally, the watchOS 11 upgrade makes the watch even easier to use, with larger icons and simplified menus.

3. Can I use the Apple Watch without an iPhone?

Yes, if you have a cellular variant of the Apple Watch Series 10, you can use many of its capabilities without needing your iPhone nearby. You can make and receive calls, send texts, and use apps like Maps, all directly from your watch.

4. How can I track my health with the Apple Watch Series 10?

The Apple Watch Series 10 delivers advanced health monitoring functions like heart rate tracking, ECG, blood oxygen levels, and fall detection. You can examine your health statistics in the Health app on your watch or your iPhone, and the watch will warn you if it detects any strange health patterns, giving you peace of mind.

5. What happens if I fall while wearing my watch?

The Apple Watch Series 10 adds Fall Detection, which identifies when you've fallen and alerts emergency personnel if you don't respond. It also sends a notification to your emergency contacts, making it an invaluable function for seniors living independently.

6. Can I change the band on my Apple Watch?

Absolutely! The Apple Watch Series 10 includes interchangeable bands, which means you may choose the band that best suits your style and comfort preferences. There are a variety of bands available, including sporty, leather, and stainless-steel alternatives.

7. Is the Apple Watch Series 10 waterproof?

Yes, the Apple Watch Series 10 is water-resistant up to 50 meters, which makes it appropriate for swimming or wearing in the shower.

This tutorial is meant to help you explore every aspect of your Apple Watch Series 10, from setting it up to mastering its features. With its comprehensive health tools, connection, and user-friendly design, this smartwatch is not just a gadget—it's a personal assistant, a health monitor, and a safety tool, all on your wrist.

We hope this tutorial empowers you to get the most out of your Apple Watch Series 10, boosting both your independence and peace of mind as you adopt this technology into your daily life.

Chapter 1

Getting Started with Apple Watch Series 10

Unboxing Your Apple Watch Series 10

When you first receive your Apple Watch Series 10, the joy of opening the box is just the beginning of your adventure into the world of smartwatches. The unboxing experience is designed to be straightforward and pleasurable, allowing you to rapidly acquaint yourself with your new gadget. Let's take a look at what you'll find when you open the box and how to get started.

The Box

The Apple device Series 10 arrives in a sleek, simple package that echoes the elegance of the device itself. As you open the box, the first thing you'll notice is the watch face and watch bands neatly placed. Apple takes considerable care in packing to ensure everything is secure and easy to access.

What's Inside the Box?

When you remove the contents of the box, here's what you'll typically find:

- **Apple Watch Series 10**: The star of the show. You'll find your Apple Watch in a separate compartment, wrapped carefully to protect it from scratches and damage. It's designed to fit comfortably on your wrist and is available in various sizes to ensure the best fit for your arm.

- **Watch Bands**: The Apple Watch comes with a band that is adjustable to different wrist sizes. The type of band you receive will depend on the model you choose (Sport Band, Leather Band, or Stainless Steel Band).

- **Charging Cable**: A USB-C charging cable, designed for safe and efficient charging, is included. This allows you to easily power your watch when it's low on battery.

- **Magnetic Charging Dock**: The Apple Watch Series 10 comes with a **magnetic charging dock**. The charging cable connects to this dock, which gently attaches to the back of your watch to charge it without the need for plugs or extra effort.

- **Documentation**: You'll also find quick-start guides and safety information, including a booklet to help you set up your device and learn more about the basics.

Now that you've unboxed your Apple Watch Series 10, it's time to dive deeper into understanding its components.

Understanding the Components

Before you begin using your new Apple Watch, it's vital to familiarize yourself with its key components. Understanding how each section works will not only make using your watch more straightforward but will also help you get the most out of its features. Let's break down the most critical elements of your Apple Watch Series 10.

The Watch Face

The watch face is the major portion of the Apple Watch you'll engage with every day. This is the screen where you can see the time, check your health stats, and access apps. Apple has built a gorgeous Retina display that reveals bright, crisp images and text, guaranteeing that you can read the display clearly, even in bright sunshine.

The watch face is customisable. You may alter it to reflect the information you need most—whether it's showing the time, weather, heart rate, or activity progress. It's designed to be visually appealing and functional at the same time.

The Digital Crown

Located on the side of the watch, the Digital Crown is an integral feature of your gadget. This little dial is used to browse through menus, zoom in on maps, and conduct other critical activities. The Digital Crown also works as a button—when clicked, it returns you back to the watch face or the Home screen. For seniors who may have problems tapping small buttons on the screen, the Digital Crown offers an alternate way to engage with your watch.

The Side Button

Next to the Digital Crown, you'll find the **side button**. This button performs several functions depending on how you press it:

- A **single press** takes you to the dock, where you can access recent apps.

- A **double press** opens the Apple Pay feature, allowing you to pay with your watch.

- Holding the side button brings up the power options, where you can power off the watch, restart it, or use the emergency SOS feature.

It's important to become familiar with this button, as it's often used for actions that go beyond just looking at the time or using apps.

The Watch Bands

The Apple Watch Series 10 comes with a **removable band**, which makes it easy to customize your watch for comfort and style. Apple offers a variety of bands for different tastes and needs:

- **Sport Band**: This band is made of soft, flexible fluoroelastomer, which is durable and resistant to sweat, making it perfect for an active lifestyle.

- **Leather Band**: A more sophisticated option, the leather band adds a touch of luxury to your watch. It's ideal for those who prefer a classic look.

- **Stainless Steel Band**: This band provides a sleek, polished look and feels premium on your wrist. It's designed for those who prefer a metal option.

You can easily swap out bands to match your outfit or comfort preferences. The **quick-release mechanism** allows you to change bands without any special tools.

The Magnetic Charging Dock and Charging Cable

To power your Apple Watch, you'll need the magnetic charging port that comes included in the package. The Apple Watch Series 10 uses MagSafe technology for charging, which is a magnetic system that allows the charging puck to automatically connect with the rear of the watch.

Once the charging puck is inserted, the watch begins to charge. A little lightning bolt icon will display on the screen to signify that the watch is charging. This technology is not just efficient but also simple to use—just place the watch on the charging station, and the magnets ensure it's perfectly positioned for charging.

The Sensors and Health Features

The back of the watch houses several **health sensors** that are responsible for tracking your heart rate, blood oxygen levels, and more. These sensors play a significant role in making the Apple

Watch Series 10 a health-focused device, providing real-time data that can help monitor and manage your well-being.

- **Heart Rate Sensor**: This sensor tracks your heart rate throughout the day and during exercise, alerting you if any abnormalities are detected.

- **ECG and Blood Oxygen Sensors**: The Apple Watch Series 10 also includes an ECG feature for monitoring heart health, as well as a blood oxygen sensor that can help detect conditions like sleep apnea or respiratory issues.

- **Fall Detection**: In addition to monitoring health, the watch has an advanced **fall detection system** that detects if you fall and can automatically alert emergency contacts if needed.

Charging Your Apple Watch Safely

Now that you understand the key components of your Apple Watch Series 10, it's time to focus on how to charge it properly and safely. Proper charging ensures that your device lasts longer and operates at optimal performance.

Step-by-Step Charging Process

To begin charging your Apple Watch, follow these simple steps:

1. **Place the Charging Dock on a Flat Surface**: Make sure the charging dock is placed on a flat surface, free from obstructions, to avoid it from falling over.

2. **Attach the Charging Cable**: Connect the charging cable to the magnetic charging dock. Ensure that the cable is plugged into a power source, such as a wall adapter or a USB port on your computer.

3. **Align the Watch with the Charging Dock**: Place the back of your Apple Watch Series 10 against the magnetic charging dock. The magnets will help automatically align the watch with the charger.

4. **Wait for the Charging Icon**: When the watch is correctly aligned and charging, a small lightning bolt icon will appear on the screen. This indicates that the charging process has begun.

Safety Tips for Charging Your Apple Watch

To ensure the longevity of your Apple Watch and avoid damage, here are some important **safety tips**:

- **Use Official Apple Chargers**: Always use the included charging dock and cable or purchase replacement accessories directly from Apple. Using third-party accessories can damage your device.

- **Charge in a Well-Ventilated Area**: Avoid charging your Apple Watch in areas that are too hot or enclosed, as excessive heat can damage the battery.

- **Don't Overcharge**: While the Apple Watch has a built-in system to prevent overcharging, it's a good idea not to leave it on the charger for too long after it reaches 100%. Unplugging the device once it's fully charged can help prolong battery health.

- **Clean the Charging Surface**: To ensure good contact between the charging dock and your watch, keep both the back of your watch and the charging surface clean. Use a soft cloth to wipe off any dust or debris before charging.

Now that you've unboxed your Apple Watch Series 10 and been comfortable with its components, it's time to start enjoying all the capabilities it has to offer. From health monitoring to bespoke bands, your Apple Watch Series 10 is designed to enhance your life in simple, yet impactful ways. Understanding how to correctly charge and care for your watch assures that it will be in outstanding shape for years to come.

Turning On and Off Your Apple Watch

Before you start using your Apple Watch Series 10, it's important to know how to turn it on and off properly. The good news is, it's very simple to do, and once you get the hang of it, you'll be able to manage the power settings with ease.

Turning On Your Apple Watch

Turning on your Apple Watch Series 10 is the first step to unlocking all the features it has to offer. Here's how to do it:

1. **Locate the Side Button**: The **side button** is the flat, round button located on the right side of the Apple Watch. It's easy to find—it's just below the Digital Crown, which we'll discuss shortly.

2. **Press and Hold the Side Button**: Press and hold the **side button** for a few seconds until you see the Apple logo appear on the screen. This indicates that the watch is powering on.

3. **Wait for the Watch to Start**: Once the Apple logo appears, the watch will begin its startup process. Depending on your settings, you may be prompted to enter your passcode or sign in with your Apple ID. If this is your first time using the watch, it will guide you through the setup process to pair the watch with your iPhone.

4. **Ready to Use**: Once the watch is fully powered on, you'll be taken to the home screen. This is where you can begin exploring the various apps and features.

Turning Off Your Apple Watch

When you're finished using your Apple Watch, it's equally important to know how to turn it off to preserve battery life and ensure the device isn't running unnecessarily. Here's how you can power off your Apple Watch:

1. **Press and Hold the Side Button**: Similar to turning on the watch, press and hold the **side button** until you see the **Power Off slider** appear on the screen.

2. **Slide to Power Off**: The screen will show a slider that says **Power Off**. Simply swipe the slider from left to right to turn off the watch.

3. **Wait for the Watch to Shut Down**: Once the watch has powered off, you'll see the screen go completely dark. This means the device is fully turned off and not consuming any battery.

4. **Restarting Your Apple Watch**: If you want to restart your Apple Watch without fully turning it off, press and hold the side button until you see the Apple logo. This will restart the watch and can help resolve any minor issues, like freezing or slow performance.

Understanding Apple Watch Buttons and Controls

To get the most out of your Apple Watch, it's essential to understand the key buttons and controls. The Apple Watch Series 10 includes two main components for interacting with your device: the **Digital Crown** and the **Side Button**.

The Digital Crown

The **Digital Crown** is located on the right side of your Apple Watch and looks like a small, round dial. It serves several functions, making it an important part of your user experience. Here's how the Digital Crown works:

- **Scroll Through Lists and Menus**: The Digital Crown is used to scroll up and down on menus or lists. For example, when you're looking through your apps or viewing messages, turning the Digital Crown will allow you to move through the options without having to touch the screen. This is particularly useful when you want to avoid smudging the screen or want to scroll through long lists quickly.

- **Zooming In and Out**: In some apps, the Digital Crown can be used to zoom in and out. For example, in the Maps app, you can turn the Digital Crown to zoom in on a map for a closer view of your location.

- **Return to the Home Screen**: Pressing the Digital Crown once will return you to the **Home Screen** (the main screen showing your apps). If you're ever lost in an app or screen, the Digital Crown is the quickest way to get back to a familiar place.

- **Accessing the App Dock**: If you press the Digital Crown twice quickly, you'll open the **App Dock**—a menu that shows your most recently used apps. This feature makes it easy to switch between apps without going back to the Home Screen.

- **Zooming In on the Watch Face**: When you're viewing your watch face, turning the Digital Crown allows you to zoom in on different complications (small widgets that show information like your heart rate, calendar events, or weather). This helps you adjust your view without needing to tap on the screen.

The Side Button

The **Side Button** is another key feature on the Apple Watch. It's located below the Digital Crown and is used for several important functions:

- **Powering On and Off**: As we discussed earlier, the Side Button is used to power on and off your Apple Watch by holding it for a few seconds.

- **Opening the Dock**: Pressing the Side Button once takes you to the **Dock**. This shows a list of your most recently used apps, making it easy to return to what you were working on.

- **Apple Pay**: Double-pressing the Side Button will activate **Apple Pay**, allowing you to make purchases directly from your watch. You'll need to have your credit or debit card set up in the Wallet app on your iPhone to use this feature.

- **Emergency SOS**: If you ever find yourself in an emergency situation, holding down the Side Button will automatically trigger the **Emergency SOS** feature. This will alert emergency services and notify your emergency contacts that you need help.

- **Setting Up and Making Calls**: You can also use the Side Button to set up a phone call when paired with your iPhone or the cellular model of the Apple Watch. Press and hold the button to prompt Siri to make calls, send texts, or manage other tasks.

Navigating with Touch, Crown, and Gestures

The Apple Watch Series 10 is designed to be straightforward and easy to use, giving a range of methods to interact with the device, from tapping and swiping to twisting the crown and utilizing hand gestures.

Each technique allows you greater flexibility over how you interact with your watch, and it's crucial to become familiar with all of them to get the most out of the device.

Using Touch to Interact with Your Watch

The touchscreen of the Apple Watch Series 10 is one of the most common ways you'll interact with your device. The display is sensitive, so even the slightest touch will register. Here's how to utilize the touchscreen effectively:

- **Tapping**: Tap on the watch face or app icons to select them. Tapping is the most common method for interacting with your watch and selecting items like messages, apps, or notifications. A single tap is all it takes to open an app or activate a function.

- **Swiping**: Swiping up, down, left, or right on the screen is used to access different menus and features. For example:

  - **Swipe Up**: This opens the **Control Center**, where you can manage settings like brightness, volume, airplane mode, and more.

- **Swipe Down**: This brings up **Notifications**, allowing you to check alerts for messages, calls, and app updates.

- **Swipe Left or Right**: This moves between different **watch faces** if you have multiple settings or allows you to move between apps on the home screen.

- **Press and Hold**: Pressing and holding on the screen (also known as a long press) will activate special features, like rearranging apps on the Home Screen or accessing settings in certain apps. For example, holding down on the watch face allows you to change it or customize it with new complications.

Using the Digital Crown for Scrolling and Zooming

As mentioned earlier, the **Digital Crown** is perfect for scrolling through long lists or zooming in on content. Here are a few specific uses:

- **Scroll Through Apps**: Use the Digital Crown to scroll through your apps on the Home Screen or the Dock. This is especially useful if you have several apps installed and need a quicker way to browse.

- **Zoom In on Maps or Photos**: The Digital Crown also works for zooming in and out on apps like Maps or Photos. When you're looking at a map or viewing an image, turning the crown will let you zoom in for more details or zoom out to get a broader view.

Gestures for Hands-Free Control

Your Apple Watch Series 10 offers several **gesture-based controls**, making it easy to interact with your device without even touching it. These gestures are particularly helpful when you're on the move or when your hands are busy:

- **Raise to Wake**: Simply raise your wrist to wake the Apple Watch screen. This gesture is especially useful when you want to check the time or notifications without touching the screen.

- **Cover to Mute**: If you receive a call or notification, you can mute the alert by covering the watch face with your hand. This is a great way to silence your watch quickly without having to press any buttons.

- **Siri Commands**: You can also interact with your Apple Watch hands-free by using **Siri**. Simply say "Hey Siri" followed by your request, and Siri will handle the task for you. Whether you want to send a text, start a workout, or check the weather, Siri makes it easy to do things without touching the watch.

Now that you've learned how to switch your Apple Watch Series 10 on and off, understand the primary buttons and controls, and navigate the watch with touch, the Digital Crown, and gestures, you're ready to start using your device.

Each of these features is meant to make your Apple Watch easy to use and interact with, whether you're simply checking the time or exploring the device's sophisticated health and communication tools.

In the following chapter, we'll go deeper into setting up your Apple Watch, syncing it with your iPhone, and personalizing your watch to suit your lifestyle.

But for now, spend some time to acquaint yourself with the buttons, controls, and gestures—these are the foundation of using your Apple Watch, and the more comfortable you grow with them, the easier it will be to enjoy everything the watch has to offer.

Chapter 2

Setting Up Your Apple Watch Series 10

Pairing Your Apple Watch with Your iPhone

The first thing you need to do when setting up your Apple Watch Series 10 is pair it with your iPhone. This step is vital, as it allows your Apple Watch to sync with your iPhone, making it possible for you to receive notifications, make calls, and use a variety of other capabilities that require a connection to your phone. Pairing the watch with your iPhone is an easy process, and with a few simple steps, you'll be linked in no time.

Step-by-Step Process to Pair Your Apple Watch with Your iPhone

1. **Ensure Your iPhone is Ready**
   Before starting the pairing process, make sure that your iPhone is updated to the latest version of iOS. This will ensure compatibility with your Apple Watch Series 10. You can check this by going to **Settings > General > Software Update** on your iPhone. If an update is available, tap **Download and Install**.

2. **Turn On Your Apple Watch**
   Once your iPhone is ready, power on your Apple Watch by pressing and holding the **Side Button** until the Apple logo appears. The watch will take a few moments to boot up.

3. **Open the Apple Watch App on Your iPhone**
   On your iPhone, open the **Apple Watch app**. This app comes pre-installed on most iPhones, but if for some reason it's not on your device, you can download it from the App Store. Once the app is open, tap **Start Pairing**.

4. **Bring the Devices Close Together**
   Hold your Apple Watch next to your iPhone, and you should see a pairing screen on your iPhone. The app will show a **viewfinder** on the screen, which you'll need to align with the **animation** on your Apple Watch. This is how the devices establish a connection.

5. **Pairing Process Begins**
   Once the camera on your iPhone scans the animation on the Apple Watch, the devices will automatically pair. You'll be asked to **agree to terms** and **set up Apple Pay** if you want to use this feature. You'll also need to **set a passcode** for your watch to secure it, as

the passcode will be required for features such as unlocking the watch and making payments.

6. **Complete the Setup**
   The setup process will guide you through a few additional steps, including **restoring from a backup** (if you had a previous Apple Watch) and **syncing apps and settings**. You'll have the option to **sync all apps** or only the essential ones. The syncing process may take a few minutes, depending on how much data needs to be transferred from your iPhone to your Apple Watch.

7. **Confirmation and Final Adjustments**
   Once the pairing process is complete, you'll receive a confirmation on both devices. Your Apple Watch will now be ready to use. You can start by customizing your watch face, choosing which notifications you'd like to receive, and setting up any additional preferences.

Language, Region, and Accessibility Settings

Once your Apple Watch is synced with your iPhone, you may alter the language, region, and accessibility settings to meet your preferences. Customizing these settings ensures that your Apple Watch works for you and makes the experience as comfortable as possible.

Changing the Language and Region

Apple offers a choice of language and regional settings to ensure your watch shows information in a way that makes sense to you. Whether you speak English, Spanish, or another language, setting your language selection is easy.

1. **Language Settings**
   To change the language on your Apple Watch, follow these steps:

   - Open the **Apple Watch app** on your iPhone.

   - Tap **General** and then select **Language & Region**.

   - Choose your preferred language from the list. The change will automatically apply to both your Apple Watch and your iPhone.

2. **Region Settings**

    Along with the language, the **region setting** ensures that your Apple Watch displays the correct time zone, date format, and regional content. To set the region:

    -   In the **Language & Region** section of the Apple Watch app, select the appropriate country or region.

    -   This will adjust the formatting for things like time (12-hour or 24-hour), date, currency, and the weather forecast for your location.

Setting Up Accessibility Features

Apple Watch is designed to be inclusive, offering a wide range of **accessibility features** that cater to people with different needs. Whether you have vision impairments, difficulty hearing, or need motor assistance, Apple Watch Series 10 includes powerful tools to help make your experience smoother and more comfortable.

Here are some key accessibility features you can adjust:

1. **VoiceOver**

    -   VoiceOver is a built-in screen reader that speaks out the text on your Apple Watch screen. This is especially useful for seniors who may have difficulty reading small text.

    -   To enable VoiceOver, go to the **Apple Watch app > Accessibility > VoiceOver** and turn on the toggle. Once activated, you can swipe or use gestures to interact with the device, and VoiceOver will read out what's on the screen.

2. **Zoom**

    -   Zoom allows you to magnify the content on your Apple Watch. If the text is too small or difficult to read, you can zoom in to get a closer look.

    -   To enable this feature, go to **Apple Watch app > Accessibility > Zoom** and toggle the feature on. Then, you can use two fingers to zoom in and out of content.

3. **Larger Text**

    ○ If you find the default text size too small, you can adjust it to make reading easier.

    ○ In the **Accessibility** menu, tap **Larger Text** and adjust the slider to increase the font size for all text displayed on your watch.

4. **Siri Voice Feedback**

    ○ If you prefer to have Siri speak feedback to you instead of displaying text, you can enable **Siri Voice Feedback** under the **Accessibility** settings. This is useful if you have difficulty reading text on the screen.

5. **Hearing Aid Compatibility**

    ○ Apple Watch Series 10 is compatible with **Made for iPhone** hearing aids. If you wear hearing aids, you can sync them with your watch to route audio directly to your devices for clearer sound.

    ○ To set this up, go to **Apple Watch app > Accessibility > Hearing Devices** and follow the instructions to pair your hearing aids with your watch.

Setting Up Wi-Fi and Bluetooth

To get the most out of your Apple Watch, you'll need to set up Wi-Fi and Bluetooth. These settings allow you to connect to the internet, sync data with your iPhone, and use additional features like music streaming and GPS tracking. Let's walk through the process of setting them up.

Setting Up Wi-Fi

1. **Ensure Your iPhone is Connected to Wi-Fi**
   Before your Apple Watch can connect to Wi-Fi, ensure that your iPhone is connected to a Wi-Fi network. This will allow your Apple Watch to sync with your phone and use features that rely on Wi-Fi, such as streaming music or checking the weather.

2. **Connect Your Apple Watch to Wi-Fi**

   ○ On your Apple Watch, swipe up from the bottom of the screen to access the **Control Center**.

   ○ Look for the **Wi-Fi icon** (it looks like a wave), and ensure that it's turned on. If it's off, tap it to enable Wi-Fi.

   ○ Once Wi-Fi is turned on, your watch will automatically connect to the same Wi-Fi network as your iPhone. If your watch doesn't detect a network, make sure your iPhone is within range and connected to Wi-Fi.

3. **Manually Connect to a Network**
   If you want to connect your Apple Watch to a different Wi-Fi network, go to **Settings > Wi-Fi** on the watch and select a network from the list of available options. You'll be prompted to enter the network's password if needed.

Setting Up Bluetooth

Bluetooth allows your Apple Watch to sync with other devices, including your iPhone, headphones, and external sensors. It's essential to have Bluetooth set up correctly to ensure full functionality of your watch.

1. **Turn On Bluetooth on Your iPhone**

   ○ Make sure that Bluetooth is enabled on your iPhone. You can do this by going to **Settings > Bluetooth**, and ensuring the toggle is turned on.

2. **Connect Apple Watch to iPhone via Bluetooth**
   When you first pair your Apple Watch with your iPhone, Bluetooth is automatically activated to ensure seamless communication between the devices. If at any point the connection drops, simply check the **Bluetooth** setting in the **Control Center** on your Apple Watch to ensure that it is enabled.

3. **Bluetooth Accessories**
   If you want to connect Bluetooth headphones or other accessories to your Apple Watch, go to **Settings > Bluetooth** on the watch and select the device from the list of available options. Once paired, you can start using the accessories with your watch.

Setting up your Apple Watch Series 10 is an exciting first step toward unlocking its full potential. By pairing it with your iPhone, changing language and accessibility options, and configuring

Wi-Fi and Bluetooth, you're creating a personalized experience that fits your lifestyle and needs. These initial steps provide the foundation for exploring all the functions that the Apple Watch Series 10 has to offer.

Configuring Notifications and Alerts

One of the most fascinating features of the Apple Watch Series 10 is its ability to keep you connected with notifications and alerts, directly from your wrist. Whether you're receiving a message, checking the weather, or getting an update on your daily activity, your Apple Watch functions as an extension of your phone, making it easier than ever to keep informed.

However, with so many apps and notifications coming through, it's crucial to set them up so that just the most critical ones are highlighted. Configuring notifications appropriately will help you stay focused on what matters most without feeling overwhelmed.

How Notifications Work on Apple Watch

By default, Apple Watch notifications mirror those of your iPhone, so you can receive the same alerts that you would on your phone—whether it's a new email, a calendar reminder, or a message from a loved one. The advantage of this approach is that you no longer have to pick up your phone to check on notifications. With a quick tap or glance, everything is right there on your wrist.

Apple Watch notifications might show as banners, alerts, or badges. The type of notification you receive depends on the app and how you arrange your settings. For example, a text message might display as a banner at the top of the screen, while a reminder might be presented as a badge on the program icon.

Customizing Notifications on Your Apple Watch

To make sure your Apple Watch is delivering notifications the way you want, it's important to adjust the settings for each app. Here's how you can do it:

1. **Open the Apple Watch App on Your iPhone**
   The Apple Watch app on your iPhone is where most of the customization happens. To access your notification settings, open the **Apple Watch app**, then tap **My Watch** at the bottom of the screen.

2. **Adjust Notifications for Individual Apps**
   Scroll down and tap on **Notifications**. This is where you can control how each app sends notifications to your watch. For each app, you can choose from the following options:

- ○ **Mirror my iPhone**: This setting ensures that the Apple Watch receives notifications in the same way as your iPhone, so if your phone alerts you to an email, your watch will do the same.

- ○ **Custom**: For apps where you want a different notification style, you can select **Custom**. This allows you to specify whether notifications are delivered as banners, alerts, or silently.

3. **Setting Alerts for Time-Sensitive Notifications**
   You can also adjust how **time-sensitive** notifications are handled. For example, if you're expecting an urgent text or a time-critical event, you can make sure those notifications are more prominent or even set them to repeat for greater visibility.

4. **Disturbances and Do Not Disturb Mode**
   If you prefer a quieter experience, you can turn on **Do Not Disturb** mode. This will silence all incoming notifications until you manually turn it off. You can find this setting under **Settings > Do Not Disturb** on your Apple Watch or within the Apple Watch app. It's useful if you don't want to be disturbed during meetings, rest, or other moments of focus.

5. **Haptic Alerts**
   One of the standout features of Apple Watch notifications is the **haptic feedback**. This feature gently taps you on the wrist to alert you of a new message, call, or reminder. You can adjust the intensity of the haptic feedback by going to **Settings > Sounds & Haptics**, and choosing the strength of the vibration. If you're someone who has trouble hearing alerts, increasing the haptic feedback ensures you don't miss important updates.

Managing Notifications and Alerts Efficiently

Managing alerts efficiently will help you prevent notification overload. If your Apple Watch feels too busy with constant alerts, you might choose to turn off notifications for specific apps, like games or entertainment apps, and keep the ones that matter most, like health updates or family messages.

A smart method is to arrange notifications by priority—keeping those for essential or time-sensitive items at the forefront, and placing less important messages on quiet or enabling them to appear only during specific hours.

Apple ID and iCloud Setup Explained Simply

Setting up your Apple ID and connecting to iCloud is vital for getting the most out of your Apple Watch. These accounts ensure that your watch is integrated into the Apple ecosystem, allowing you to sync your apps, settings, and data easily between devices. Plus, having your Apple ID and iCloud set up properly enables several of the most crucial features on the Apple Watch, such as Find My, iCloud backup, and more.

What is Apple ID?

Your Apple ID is effectively your own account with Apple, providing you access to the complete range of services the firm offers. You'll use your Apple ID to access the App Store, iCloud, Apple Music, and other Apple services. Without an Apple ID, your Apple Watch won't be able to fully connect with the features Apple has designed for smooth use across various devices.

Setting Up Apple ID on Your Apple Watch

To set up your Apple ID on your Apple Watch Series 10, follow these simple steps:

1. **On Your iPhone**
   Ensure that you are signed in to **iCloud** with your Apple ID on your iPhone. Go to **Settings** and tap your name at the top of the screen to view your Apple ID settings. If you're not signed in, tap **Sign In to Your iPhone** and enter your Apple ID and password.

2. **Link Apple ID to Your Apple Watch**
   When pairing your Apple Watch to your iPhone (as outlined in Chapter 1), you will be prompted to sign in with your Apple ID. Follow the on-screen instructions to enter your Apple ID credentials, and your watch will sync with your iCloud account. This will ensure that all your contacts, calendars, and apps are readily available on your Apple Watch.

Setting Up iCloud

iCloud is a cloud-based storage service from Apple that lets you securely store your photos, documents, and other important data online. When you set up iCloud on your Apple Watch, your data is backed up, meaning that if your watch gets lost or replaced, you can easily restore your settings, apps, and data to your new device.

Here's how to set up iCloud on your Apple Watch:

1. **Sign In to iCloud on Your iPhone**
   Open **Settings** on your iPhone and tap **[your name] > iCloud**. Make sure you're signed

in with your Apple ID. Toggle on the apps and services that you want to sync with iCloud. For example, you can sync **Contacts**, **Calendars**, **Reminders**, and more.

2. **Enable iCloud Syncing for Apple Watch**

   When you set up your Apple Watch, iCloud syncing is automatically enabled. This means that the data you store in iCloud will be accessible on your watch, such as calendar events, messages, reminders, and more.

3. **iCloud Backup**

   iCloud also automatically backs up your Apple Watch's settings and app data, ensuring that even if your watch is replaced or reset, you can restore your information from iCloud. To check if iCloud backup is enabled, go to **Settings > [your name] > iCloud > iCloud Backup** on your iPhone.

Updating to the Latest watchOS 11

Keeping your Apple Watch updated to the latest version of watchOS 11 guarantees that you have access to the newest features, upgrades, and security updates. watchOS 11 brings various changes, from new watch faces to increased health features and smarter notifications. Updating your Apple Watch is straightforward and takes only a few minutes, ensuring your device continues to perform effortlessly.

Why You Should Update to watchOS 11

With every new version of watchOS, Apple adds important enhancements to the system, including:

- **Improved health features**: Enhanced monitoring tools for heart rate, sleep tracking, and even new apps designed to help you stay healthy and fit.

- **Faster performance**: Updates often include under-the-hood improvements that make your Apple Watch run more smoothly and efficiently.

- **New watch faces and customization options**: With watchOS 11, you can personalize your watch more than ever, choosing watch faces that best fit your needs and style.

- **Bug fixes and security updates**: Keeping your watchOS up to date ensures that your Apple Watch is protected against any security threats.

How to Update Your Apple Watch to watchOS 11

To update your Apple Watch to the latest version of watchOS 11, follow these steps:

1. **Check for the Update**
   Make sure your Apple Watch is connected to your iPhone and has at least **50% battery life**. The update process requires both a connection to the internet and sufficient power.

2. **Start the Update**
   Open the **Apple Watch app** on your iPhone, then tap **General > Software Update**. If an update is available, you will see a notification. Tap **Download and Install** to begin the update process.

3. **Install the Update**
   Your Apple Watch will begin downloading the update. Once it's done, it will automatically begin installing. You'll see a progress bar on the screen of your Apple Watch. Once the update is complete, your watch will restart, and the new features of watchOS 11 will be available.

4. **Automatic Updates**
   If you prefer, you can enable **automatic updates** for watchOS, ensuring your device updates itself in the background when new versions are released. To enable automatic updates, go to **Settings > General > Software Update** on your iPhone and toggle on **Automatic Updates**.

What to Do If You Encounter Issues During the Update

If you experience any issues during the update, such as slow download speeds or errors during installation, try the following troubleshooting steps:

- **Check Your Internet Connection**: Ensure your iPhone is connected to a reliable Wi-Fi network. A slow or unstable connection can interrupt the update.

- **Restart Your Devices**: Restart both your iPhone and Apple Watch and try the update again.

- **Free Up Space**: If your Apple Watch is low on storage, you may need to free up space before the update will install. You can manage storage by going to **Settings > General > Usage** on your Apple Watch.

Setting up your Apple Watch Series 10 is an exciting process, and now that you know how to set up notifications and alerts, set up your Apple ID and iCloud, and upgrade your watch to the current version of watchOS 11, you're well on your way to enjoying everything the watch has to offer. Each of these settings ensures that your Apple Watch is personalized and performing properly, allowing you to stay connected, stay healthy, and get the most out of your device.

Chapter 3

Understanding the Apple Watch Interface

The Home Screen Layout and Dock

The Apple Watch Series 10 is designed to be simple and straightforward, making it easy to interact with even if you've never used a wristwatch before. One of the first things you'll meet on your Apple Watch is the Home Screen—this is where you'll find all your apps and tools, exactly like the Home Screen on an iPhone. But it's not just about the apps; understanding the style and arrangement of the Home Screen is crucial to getting the most out of your Apple Watch.

What is the Home Screen?

The Home Screen of the Apple Watch is the main interface where you can access all your apps and functionality. It's where you'll go to check the clock, see notifications, and open the apps you need. You can think of it as the beginning point for all your actions on the Apple Watch.

There are two main ways to interact with the Home Screen:

- **Grid View**: This is the default view for most Apple Watch users. In Grid View, apps are displayed in a grid-like layout, with circular icons for each app. It's visually appealing and allows you to quickly scan your apps at a glance.

- **List View**: If you prefer a more organized view, you can switch to List View. This mode displays your apps in a vertical list, with their names written next to each app icon. List View is especially useful if you have many apps and want to see them all clearly, without any overlap.

How to Change the Home Screen Layout

To change between **Grid View** and **List View**, follow these steps:

1. Press the **Digital Crown** to open the Home Screen.

2. **Force press** (press firmly) on the Home Screen until you see a menu appear.

3. Tap **GridView** or **Listview** to choose the layout that works best for you.

Both positions have their advantages, but the choice ultimately rests on what seems most comfortable to you. Whether you want a cleaner, more structured list or a colorful, icon-based display, the Apple Watch offers options.

The Dock: Quick Access to Your Favorite Apps

The Dock on the Apple Watch is a feature that allows you to instantly access the apps you use most often, without having to scroll through the Home Screen. Think of it as a shortcut to your favorite tools. You can put up to 10 apps in the Dock, making it quick to navigate between your most-used functions with a simple swipe.

The Dock is accessed by pressing the **Side Button,** located directly below the Digital Crown. When you touch the Side Button, a list of your recent apps will appear on the screen. You may easily scroll through the list and press on an app to open it.

You can manage which apps appear in the Dock by following these steps:

1. **Press the Side Button** to open the Dock.

2. Scroll to the bottom and tap **Edit**.

3. You'll see a list of apps that you can add or remove from the Dock. Tap the red **minus** button to remove an app, or tap the green **plus** button to add a new app.

4. Once you're finished, tap **Done** to save your changes.

The Dock is a great way to keep your favorite apps easily accessible and avoid the need to dig through the Home Screen every time you want to open something.

Using the Digital Crown and Side Button

The **Digital Crown** and **Side Button** are two essential controls on your Apple Watch Series 10. Understanding how and when to use these buttons will make it easier to interact with your device and access all its features. Let's take a closer look at each of these controls.

The Digital Crown: Your Multi-Purpose Control

The **Digital Crown** is a round dial located on the right side of the Apple Watch. It may look simple, but it's one of the most versatile buttons on the device, serving a variety of functions. Here's how you can use the Digital Crown:

1. **Scrolling**

   The Digital Crown is perfect for scrolling through menus and lists. Whether you're going through apps, reading messages, or reviewing your fitness stats, turning the Digital Crown will move you up or down a list. This is especially helpful for navigating through long pages or seeing all your data at once without having to touch the screen.

2. **Zooming In and Out**

   In some apps, such as **Maps** or **Photos**, the Digital Crown allows you to zoom in and out. You can rotate the Crown to get a closer look at a location or image, which is much easier than trying to pinch and zoom on the small screen.

3. **Returning to the Home Screen**

   One of the most useful functions of the Digital Crown is its ability to return you to the Home Screen. Press the Digital Crown once, and you'll be taken back to the main screen where all your apps are located. This is a quick way to escape any app and start fresh.

4. **Switching Between Apps**

   The Digital Crown also lets you **switch between apps**. By pressing it twice quickly, you'll see the **App Switcher**, which shows your recently used apps. You can then scroll through this list and tap on any app to open it.

5. **Adjusting Volume**

   If you're listening to music, a podcast, or using the Siri voice assistant, you can use the Digital Crown to adjust the volume. Simply turn the Crown up or down to increase or decrease the sound.

The Side Button: A Multi-Functional Control

The **Side Button** is located just below the Digital Crown. Though it might look simple, it has several important functions that make it indispensable for everyday use. Here's how the Side Button works:

1. **Powering On and Off**

   If your Apple Watch is turned off, press and hold the Side Button to power it on. If you want to turn off your watch, press and hold the Side Button again until the **Power Off slider** appears. Slide it to turn off the device.

2. **Accessing the Dock**

   Press the Side Button once to bring up the **Dock**, which shows your most recently used apps. The Dock is a convenient way to switch between apps quickly without having to go back to the Home Screen.

3. **Activating Apple Pay**

   Double-click the Side Button to activate **Apple Pay**. This feature allows you to make secure payments with your watch, using your linked credit or debit card. Simply hold the watch near a payment terminal, and it will process the transaction for you.

4. **Emergency SOS**

   In case of an emergency, press and hold the Side Button to activate the **Emergency SOS** feature. This will call emergency services and notify your emergency contacts that you need help. This is a crucial safety feature that can be life-saving in urgent situations.

5. **Taking Screenshots**

   The Side Button can also be used to take a screenshot of what's currently on your screen. Press the Side Button and Digital Crown at the same time to capture an image. This is useful if you want to save something on your watch for later reference.

Customizing Watch Faces (Step-by-Step Guide)

One of the most exciting features of the Apple Watch is the option to customize your watch face. The watch face is the first thing you see when you raise your wrist, so it's crucial to make it appear and feel like your own. Whether you choose a clean, minimalist look or a vivid, data-packed display, Apple Watch gives you limitless options to personalize your watch face.

Why Customize Your Watch Face?

Customizing your watch face allows you to:

- **Showcase your personal style**: Choose from a variety of designs that reflect your personality, whether you prefer something simple or bold.

- **Stay organized**: Add complications (small widgets) to your watch face to see the information that matters most to you, such as weather, heart rate, or upcoming appointments.

- **Set the mood**: You can adjust your watch face to match the time of day, season, or even your outfit.

How to Customize Your Watch Face

Here's a step-by-step guide to customizing your Apple Watch Series 10's watch face:

1. **Press the Digital Crown** to go to the Home Screen.

2. **Press and Hold the Watch Face**
   On the Home Screen, press and hold the watch face. This will put your watch into **edit mode**, allowing you to change the look and feel of your watch face.

3. **Swipe Through Watch Faces**
   If you want to switch to a different watch face, swipe left or right. You'll see a variety of faces, including **Utility, Modular, Infographic,** and more. Tap on the one you like to set as your new watch face.

4. **Customize Your Watch Face**
   To customize the selected watch face, tap **Customize**. From here, you can adjust various elements:

   - **Color**: Some watch faces allow you to change the color of the background or complications. Simply swipe to change the color palette.

   - **Complications**: These are the small widgets on your watch face that provide quick access to information like the date, weather, or activity status. Tap on the complication you want to change, and scroll the Digital Crown to select a new option.

   - **Style**: Some watch faces offer different styles, such as analog, digital, or hybrid, which you can choose based on your preference.

5. **Save Your Changes**
   Once you've made all your adjustments, press the **Digital Crown** to save your changes and return to the Home Screen. Your new watch face is now set.

Adding More Watch Faces

If you want to add even more options to your watch faces, you can do so from the **Apple Watch app** on your iPhone. Here's how:

1. Open the **Apple Watch app** on your iPhone.

2. Tap **Face Gallery** at the bottom of the screen.

3. Browse through the available faces and tap the one you like to add it to your Apple Watch.

4. Tap **Add** to save it.

Now you can easily switch between a variety of watch faces depending on your mood or the time of day.

Complications: What They Are and How to Use Them

One of the most distinctive and helpful features of the Apple Watch Series 10 is the option to customize your watch face using complications. But what precisely are complexities, and how might they enhance your experience with the watch?

What Are Complications?

In the realm of watches, complications relate to small pieces of supplementary information displayed on the watch face, beyond the basic time. On the Apple Watch Series 10, complications may display everything from your current heart rate, battery life, and weather updates, to upcoming calendar events, or even your daily activity progress.

Complications are highly versatile, as they allow you to modify your watch face to convey the information that's most essential to you. For example, if you're someone who likes to be active, you could want a complication that shows your activity rings. If you rely on your watch for weather updates, you might choose a complication that shows the current temperature. No matter what you need to keep track of, complexities provide you easy access to the information you use most.

How to Add and Customize Complications

Adding and customizing complications on your Apple Watch Series 10 is a straightforward process. Here's how you can do it:

1. **Choose Your Watch Face**
   First, make sure you're on the Home Screen of your Apple Watch by pressing the **Digital Crown**. If you are on a watch face that you want to customize, press and hold the screen until you enter **Edit Mode**.

2. **Tap on Customize**

   Once you've entered Edit Mode, tap **Customize** to begin adjusting your watch face settings. You'll see the option to adjust different elements of the face, including the complications.

3. **Swipe to the Complication Area**

   Use the **Digital Crown** to scroll to the complication areas of the watch face. You'll see different spots on the watch where complications can be placed. Some watch faces allow you to add complications in multiple areas, such as the **top**, **bottom**, or **corners**.

4. **Select a Complication**

   Tap on a complication spot to see a list of available options. These options will vary depending on the watch face you are using. You'll find complications related to fitness, health, weather, music, and much more. Scroll through the list using the **Digital Crown** and tap on the one you want to add.

5. **Adjust and Save**

   Once you've chosen your complications, press the **Digital Crown** to save your settings. Your customized watch face, complete with your selected complications, will now be active.

Types of Complications

There are several types of complications that you can choose from, and understanding what each one offers can help you create a personalized watch face suited to your needs.

- **Health and Fitness Complications**: These include **activity rings** (to track your movement, exercise, and standing progress), **heart rate**, **calories burned**, and **sleep tracking**.

- **Weather Complications**: You can add complications that show **current temperature**, **forecast**, and **humidity**.

- **Time and Date Complications**: Some complications show the **day of the week**, **date**, or even offer a **countdown timer** for an upcoming event.

- **Battery Life**: This complication shows the remaining battery percentage, helping you keep track of how much longer your watch will last before needing to charge.

- **Quick Access to Apps**: You can also add complications that link to specific apps, such as **Calendar**, **Messages**, or **Music**, for easy access.

Using Complications Effectively

The key to employing complexities efficiently is personalizing them to match your specific needs. If you're someone who loves to measure your physical activity, emphasizing fitness complications like the activity rings and heart rate will help you keep on top of your health goals. On the other hand, if you routinely check the weather, you could choose to add the weather complication.

Additionally, keep in mind that complexities might impact how much information is shown on your watch face. For a cleaner, more streamlined look, you might choose fewer complexities, while a more information-dense watch face could have many complications for things like weather, calendar events, and fitness tracking. It's all about finding the proper balance for you.

Control Center and Quick Access Features

The Control Center is another important function on the Apple Watch Series 10 that allows you to quickly access essential settings without having to dig through menus or apps. The Control Center allows you the power to make adjustments to your device in seconds, which is very beneficial if you're in a rush or need to modify something quickly.

What is the Control Center?

Think of the Control Center as a shortcut to some of the most regularly used settings on your Apple Watch. Whether you need to modify your volume, brightness, or Wi-Fi, the Control Center gives you simple access to all these settings and more.

You may open the Control Center by swiping up from the bottom of the screen. Once you do, you'll see a range of symbols representing different options. These options are split into categories, and each icon has a specific function.

Control Center Functions and Icons

Here are some of the key icons you'll find in the Control Center, and what each of them does:

1. **Airplane Mode**
   This icon looks like an airplane and allows you to turn on **Airplane Mode**. When enabled, Airplane Mode disables all wireless communications, such as Wi-Fi, Bluetooth, and cellular, which can be helpful when you're flying or simply need to disconnect from your devices.

2. **Do Not Disturb**

This icon is a crescent moon. When **Do Not Disturb** is enabled, your Apple Watch will stop all notifications, calls, and alerts. This is especially useful when you need to focus or get some quiet time without interruptions.

3. **Silent Mode**

This icon looks like a bell with a slash through it. Turning on **Silent Mode** mutes your Apple Watch, so you won't hear notifications or alerts, though the haptic feedback (vibration) will still occur.

4. **Battery Percentage**

This icon shows the **battery percentage** left on your Apple Watch. If your battery is low, you can tap the icon to access more power settings or activate **Power Reserve Mode**.

5. **Wi-Fi and Bluetooth**

These two icons allow you to quickly access your watch's **Wi-Fi** and **Bluetooth** settings. If you need to disconnect from a network or connect to a new device, this is the quickest way to do it.

6. **Theater Mode**

The **Theater Mode** icon looks like two masks (theater masks). When enabled, this mode silences your watch and disables the "Raise to Wake" feature, meaning the screen won't light up when you lift your wrist. This is useful when you're in a movie or any setting where you don't want your watch to disturb others.

7. **Ping iPhone**

If you ever misplace your iPhone, you can use the **Ping iPhone** feature to make your iPhone play a sound, even if it's on silent. This is especially helpful if your phone is nearby but out of sight.

Quick Access to Settings

The Control Center is also a fast way to access some common settings on the Apple Watch, such as:

- **Adjusting brightness**: Slide the brightness slider to make the screen brighter or dimmer based on your preference.

- **Changing volume**: Use the volume slider to adjust the sound level for alerts, calls, and media.

- **Toggling Wi-Fi or Bluetooth**: Turn Wi-Fi or Bluetooth on or off with a single tap.

How to Customize the Control Center

If there are specific features you use more frequently, you can customize the Control Center to make it even more convenient. To add or remove items:

1. Open the **Apple Watch app** on your iPhone.

2. Tap **My Watch** and then **Control Center**.

3. From here, you can toggle on or off the options you'd like to appear in the Control Center.

Using Siri – Your Voice Assistant

Siri, Apple's speech assistant, is a powerful tool that can help you accomplish everything from setting reminders and sending emails to checking the weather and controlling smart home gadgets. With Siri, you can use your voice to get things done without lifting a finger—perfect for when your hands are full or when you simply want a speedier way to communicate with your Apple Watch.

How to Activate Siri

There are several ways to activate Siri on your Apple Watch, depending on how you prefer to use the feature:

1. **Hey Siri**
   Simply say the phrase **"Hey Siri"**, and Siri will respond to your command. This hands-free method is perfect if you don't want to press any buttons.

2. **Press and Hold the Digital Crown**
   If you prefer to use a button, press and hold the **Digital Crown** for a few seconds. Siri will appear on the screen and be ready to take your command.

3. **Raise to Speak**
   On some models of Apple Watch, you can enable **Raise to Speak**, which allows you to speak to Siri simply by raising your wrist. When this feature is activated, Siri will automatically respond when you lift your wrist and speak your command.

What Siri Can Do

Siri on your Apple Watch is capable of performing a wide range of tasks, including:

- **Setting Reminders and Alarms**: Simply tell Siri, "Set a reminder to take my medication at 2 PM," or "Set an alarm for 6 AM."

- **Sending Messages**: "Send a message to John saying, 'I'll be there in 10 minutes.'"

- **Checking Weather and Sports**: "What's the weather like today?" or "What's the score of the game?"

- **Making Calls**: "Call Mom" or "Dial Sarah."

- **Controlling Smart Home Devices**: If you have smart home devices connected through HomeKit, you can use Siri to control lights, thermostats, and other smart appliances. "Turn off the living room lights," for example.

- **Starting a Workout**: "Start a walking workout" or "Track my yoga session."

Customizing Siri

To adjust how Siri interacts with your Apple Watch, follow these steps:

1. Open the **Apple Watch app** on your iPhone.

2. Tap **My Watch**, then tap **Siri**.

3. From here, you can customize settings like enabling **Raise to Speak**, adjusting voice feedback, or changing Siri's language.

Understanding how to use the complexities, Control Center, and Siri on your Apple Watch Series 10 can enhance your experience and make it easier to access the information and services you need most. Whether you're personalizing your watch face, quickly modifying settings, or using your voice to engage with Siri, these tools are meant to make your watch even more personal and efficient.

Chapter 4

Staying Connected: Calls, Messages & Notifications

Making and Receiving Calls from Your Wrist

One of the striking features of the Apple Watch Series 10 is its ability to let you make and receive calls straight from your wrist. This is especially beneficial for seniors who might find it difficult to reach for their phone, or for those instances when your phone is across the room, buried in your luggage, or even charging in another room. With your Apple Watch, you can stay connected effortlessly.

Making Calls from Your Apple Watch

Making calls on your Apple Watch is incredibly simple and quick. The best part? You don't need to touch your phone at all. Here's how to make a call from your wrist:

1. **Using the Phone App on Your Watch**
   The **Phone app** on your Apple Watch allows you to make calls to anyone in your contacts list. Here's how to use it:

   ○ Press the **Digital Crown** to open the Home Screen and locate the **Phone app** (the icon looks like a green phone).

   ○ Tap the **Phone app** to open it.

   ○ You'll see three tabs at the bottom of the screen: **Favorites**, **Recents**, and **Contacts**. Choose one of these tabs to find the person you want to call.

   ○ Tap on the contact's name, and then select the **phone icon** to make the call. If you have a **cellular model** of the Apple Watch, you can make the call directly from the watch without needing your phone.

2. **Using Siri to Make Calls**
   Another quick way to make a call is by using **Siri**, your voice assistant. Just say **"Hey Siri"**, followed by the name of the person you want to call, and Siri will place the call for you. For example, you can say, "Hey Siri, call Mom" or "Hey Siri, dial Sarah."

3. **Making Calls via Bluetooth Headset or Speaker**
   If you prefer a hands-free calling experience, you can pair a **Bluetooth headset** or use the **speakerphone** on your Apple Watch. Once the call is connected, simply speak into the watch or use your Bluetooth headset to communicate.

Receiving Calls on Your Apple Watch

Receiving calls on the Apple Watch is just as easy. If you're wearing your watch, you'll feel a subtle **haptic vibration** when you receive a call, making it easy to know when someone is trying to reach you. Here's what to do when you get a call:

1. **Answering a Call**
   When the call comes in, you'll see the caller's name (if they're in your contacts) or the number displayed on your watch screen. To answer, simply tap the green **Answer** button. You can then use your watch's built-in **speaker** to talk to the caller or connect a **Bluetooth headset** for a clearer conversation.

2. **Declining a Call**
   If you're unable to take the call, swipe the red **Decline** button. Alternatively, you can press the **Side Button** to send the caller to voicemail.

3. **Using the Speaker or Bluetooth**
   Your Apple Watch Series 10 lets you decide how you want to hear and speak during calls. You can use the built-in speaker for hands-free calling, or connect a **Bluetooth headset** for better sound quality. You'll also find a **mute** button on the call screen, which allows you to silence your side of the conversation if needed.

4. **Hands-Free Options**
   With **Apple CarPlay** (if you have a compatible car), you can even answer calls directly from your car's display without having to touch your Apple Watch.

Using the Apple Watch for Conference Calls and Group Chats

Another excellent feature of the Apple Watch Series 10 is the ability to join conference calls or group chats, making it easy to stay connected with multiple people at once. Whether it's a business call or a family chat, you can join in right from your wrist.

- For **conference calls**, simply join the call as you normally would, and you can switch between participants or mute yourself directly from your watch.

- For **group chats** via messaging apps, you can stay in touch with multiple people at once and quickly respond to group messages.

Sending Text Messages and Emojis

Sending messages is one of the most common activities on your Apple Watch. Whether you're replying to a text from a loved one or sending a quick note to a friend, your watch makes it easy to communicate without needing to pull out your phone.

Sending a Text Message via the Messages App

1. **Accessing the Messages App**
   Open the **Messages app** on your Apple Watch by pressing the **Digital Crown** and selecting the **Messages icon** (it looks like a speech bubble). You'll see a list of all your recent conversations.

2. **Replying to a Message**
   When you tap on a message, you'll be able to read it and then respond. There are several ways to reply, depending on your preferences:

   o **Quick Reply**: If you want to send a quick reply, you can use the **predefined responses** in the watch. These are short messages like "Okay," "Thanks," or "Talk later." Simply tap on the response you want to send, and it will be delivered.

   o **Dictation**: You can **speak your reply** by tapping the **microphone** button on the message screen. Speak your message, and Siri will transcribe it for you.

   o **Emoji**: You can also send emojis by tapping the **emoji icon** and choosing from a wide range of expressive images. Whether it's a smiley face, a thumbs up, or a heart, emojis make it fun and easy to convey your emotions in a message.

3. **Using Scribble to Type a Message**
   If you prefer typing, you can use **Scribble**. This allows you to write each letter of the message directly on the screen using your finger. The Apple Watch will automatically convert your handwriting into text. To use Scribble, just tap on the **Text** field in the Messages app, and then start writing the letters of your message one at a time. The Apple Watch will convert your scribbled letters into words, making it easy to send a personalized message.

Sending and Receiving Emojis

Emojis have become an essential part of communication, allowing us to express emotions, reactions, and ideas in a fun and visual way. With the Apple Watch, sending emojis is just as easy as sending text.

1. **Sending Emojis**
   When replying to a message, you can tap the **emoji icon** to open a selection of emojis. Scroll through the available options using the **Digital Crown**, and then tap on the emoji you want to send. You can also use **Siri** to insert emojis by simply saying, "Send a happy face emoji to John."

2. **Receiving Emojis**
   If you receive an emoji in a message, you'll see it displayed on your screen along with the text. When replying, you can send your own emoji in response. Emojis are a fun way to make communication feel more personal and engaging.

3. **Using Emoji Suggestions**
   As you type a message using **Scribble** or **Dictation**, the Apple Watch will often suggest emojis that match the context of your message. For example, if you type "Thank you," it might suggest a thumbs-up emoji or a heart emoji to accompany your text.

Using Dictation and Scribble for Text

Dictation and Scribble are two powerful features of the Apple Watch Series 10 that make text entry quick and easy, especially for seniors who may find typing on a small screen difficult.

Dictation: Speak Your Message

Dictation allows you to dictate your message, and Siri will automatically transcribe it for you. This is perfect for seniors who may have difficulty typing on small keyboards, as it allows for quick and efficient communication.

1. **Using Dictation**
   When composing a message, tap the **microphone icon** on the screen. This activates **Siri Dictation**, allowing you to speak your message out loud. For example, say "Hi, how are you today?" and your watch will convert it into text.

2. **Adding Punctuation**

    You can also dictate punctuation marks to make your messages more natural. Simply say "comma," "period," "question mark," or "exclamation point," and Siri will add the correct punctuation to your message.

3. **Correcting Mistakes**

    If Siri misunderstands a word, you can tap the word and correct it manually. You can also use voice commands like "Delete that" to remove unwanted text or "Insert [word]" to add text where needed.

4. **Using Dictation for Multiple Languages**

    Siri supports multiple languages, so you can dictate messages in your preferred language. If you speak more than one language, Siri will understand and transcribe the message in the language you are speaking.

Scribble: Write Your Message by Hand

Scribble is another excellent way to send messages on the Apple Watch, allowing you to draw each letter of the message with your finger. It's a great option for those who prefer the tactile feel of writing over speaking.

1. **Using Scribble**

    To use Scribble, tap the **Text** field in the Messages app and start writing the letters of your message one by one. As you write, your letters will be converted into text in real time. You can write simple messages, such as "Hello," or more complex ones, and the watch will automatically recognize your handwriting.

2. **Using Scribble for Emojis**

    You can also use Scribble to draw emojis. Simply tap the **emoji icon**, and Scribble will allow you to write out an emoji by sketching it. For example, you can draw a smiley face or a heart, and the Apple Watch will recognize the drawing and convert it into emoji.

3. **Adjusting Scribble Settings**

    If you have trouble using Scribble, you can adjust the settings to make it easier. Go to **Settings > Accessibility** and adjust the settings for **Scribble**. You can change the sensitivity and speed of the feature to match your preferences.

Staying connected has never been easier with the Apple Watch Series 10. Whether you're making and receiving calls, sending text messages with emojis, or using the voice-powered Siri assistant to connect, your Apple Watch is designed to keep you in contact with family, friends, and the world around you. With tools like Dictation and Scribble, messaging is quick and straightforward, and you can even express yourself more creatively with emojis.

Managing Notifications – Don't Miss What Matters

In today's fast-paced world, alerts are a crucial component of staying connected. However, with so many apps and communications streaming in, it can be daunting to handle everything. The Apple Watch Series 10 helps you manage your alerts in a way that allows you to remain on top of what's important while avoiding unwanted distractions. Let's discuss how you may make the most of this function, ensuring that you only get notified about what genuinely matters.

What Are Notifications on Your Apple Watch?

Notifications on your Apple Watch Series 10 alert you to new messages, calendar events, social media updates, and much more. They are supposed to keep you informed and connected, but they can also become overwhelming if you receive too many.

When a new notification comes in, your Apple Watch will vibrate gently (thanks to its haptic feedback) and display the alert on the screen. You'll notice the sort of notification, whether it's a text message, email, reminder, or app notification. For many elderly, the mild vibration is enough to draw attention without being obtrusive.

However, you don't need to be overwhelmed by every app delivering notifications. With Apple Watch, you can simply configure and control which notifications you want to receive and how you want them to look.

How to Manage Notifications on Your Apple Watch

To make sure your Apple Watch is only sending you relevant notifications, here's how you can adjust the settings:

1. **Open the Apple Watch App**
   Start by opening the **Apple Watch app** on your iPhone. This app is where you will manage most of the settings for your Apple Watch.

2. **Tap on Notifications**
   In the Apple Watch app, tap **Notifications**. Here, you'll see a list of all the apps on your watch that are capable of sending notifications.

3. **Customize App Notifications**

   For each app, you can choose whether to receive notifications at all or whether to mirror your iPhone's settings. For example, you can choose to receive **email notifications**, but only for important senders, or turn off notifications from apps like games, which may be less important to you.

4. **Adjust How Notifications Appear**

   Apple Watch lets you adjust how notifications are displayed on your screen. You can choose to show them as **banners**, which appear briefly at the top of your screen, or as **alerts**, which require you to take action. Additionally, you can set how your watch handles **repeated alerts**—whether they should repeat if you don't respond or only show once.

5. **Silent Notifications**

   If you want to stay aware of incoming messages or updates but don't want your watch to vibrate every time, you can set **silent notifications**. This way, the alert will appear on the screen, but it won't vibrate or make a sound. This is especially useful during meetings or at night when you want to avoid distractions but still want to keep an eye on important updates.

6. **Using Do Not Disturb**

   The **Do Not Disturb** feature allows you to silence all notifications when you need some quiet time, like during a meeting, at the movies, or when you're sleeping. You can enable Do Not Disturb through the **Control Center** by swiping up from the bottom of the watch screen. Once activated, all alerts, sounds, and vibrations will be silenced.

7. **Customizing Do Not Disturb**

   You can customize **Do Not Disturb** settings to allow specific notifications to come through, such as **calls from family members** or **important reminders**. This is useful for seniors who want to avoid interruptions but still be available for crucial calls or messages.

8. **Priority Notifications**

   If you receive a lot of notifications but only care about a few (such as family texts, doctor appointments, or work-related updates), you can adjust your settings to prioritize those specific notifications. You can do this by assigning a **priority** to certain apps or contacts within your notification settings, ensuring that only the most important updates grab your attention.

Taking Action on Notifications

When you receive a notification, you have several ways to respond or take action directly from your Apple Watch:

- **Swipe Down to View Details**: Swipe down on the notification to reveal more information. For example, if you get a message or email notification, you can see a preview of the message right on your wrist.

- **Tap to Open**: If the notification requires further action (like replying to a text or checking an event), tap on the notification, and it will open the associated app.

- **Clear Notifications**: You can swipe left on notifications to dismiss them. This keeps your watch screen free from unnecessary alerts and ensures that only current notifications remain.

Using Mail, Calendar, and Reminders

Your Apple Watch Series 10 is not just for fitness monitoring and communication—it's also a terrific tool for planning your day and keeping track of your responsibilities. With built-in apps like Mail, Calendar, and Reminders, your watch becomes a crucial element of managing your personal and professional life. Let's investigate how you can use these features successfully.

Using Mail on Your Apple Watch

The **Mail app** on your Apple Watch allows you to stay on top of your email right from your wrist. You can read new emails, mark them as read, and even reply—all without needing to pull out your phone.

Here's how to use the Mail app on your Apple Watch:

1. **Open the Mail App**
   Press the **Digital Crown** to access the Home Screen and tap on the **Mail app** (the envelope icon). You'll be able to see a list of all your inboxes and emails that have arrived.

2. **Reading Emails**
   Tap on an email to read it. Your watch will display a preview of the message, allowing you to quickly skim through the content. You can also scroll up and down through the message if it's long.

3. **Replying to Emails**

   To reply to an email, tap on **Reply**. You can then choose how to respond:

   - **Dictation**: Use **Siri** to speak your response. Your Apple Watch will transcribe your speech into text and send the email.

   - **Predefined Replies**: Tap on one of the quick reply options to send a short, predefined message. You can choose from responses like "Thanks!" or "I'll get back to you soon."

   - **Emojis**: You can also send emojis in your email responses, making your messages more personal and expressive.

4. **Marking Emails**

   If you don't need to reply right away but want to keep track of an email, you can mark it as **read**, **flag it**, or **move it to a folder**. These actions can be done directly from your Apple Watch without needing to open your iPhone.

Using Calendar to Stay Organized

The **Calendar app** on your Apple Watch helps you keep track of appointments, meetings, and events. It syncs directly with the Calendar app on your iPhone, so you'll always have the latest information.

Here's how to use the Calendar app effectively:

1. **Viewing Events**

   Tap on the **Calendar app** from the Home Screen of your Apple Watch. You'll see a list of your events for the day or week, depending on how you prefer to view them. You can scroll through the list and tap on any event to see more details.

2. **Adding New Events**

   To add a new event, tap on the **+ icon** (if enabled). This will open a window where you can dictate or scribble the event details, such as the title, time, and location. Your Apple Watch will sync this event with your iPhone's Calendar app, ensuring that both devices are up-to-date.

3. **Getting Event Alerts**

   The Calendar app will send you notifications before your events, keeping you on track and organized. You can adjust these notifications based on your preferences, so you never miss an important meeting, doctor's appointment, or social event.

Using Reminders for Task Management

The **Reminders app** on your Apple Watch is the perfect tool for organizing your tasks and to-do lists. Whether you need to be reminded to take your medication, call a family member, or pick up groceries, the Reminders app can help you stay on top of things.

Here's how you can use the Reminders app effectively:

1. **Creating New Reminders**
   To create a reminder, open the **Reminders app** from the Home Screen and tap the + **icon**. You can dictate or use the Scribble feature to type out the task. You can set specific times or dates for reminders, so they alert you when you need to take action.

2. **Checking Off Tasks**
   Once you've completed a task, you can quickly check it off directly from your Apple Watch. Simply tap the task in the list, and the checkbox will appear. Tap it to mark the task as completed.

3. **Setting Location-Based Reminders**
   One of the powerful features of the Reminders app is the ability to set **location-based reminders**. For example, you can create a reminder that says, "Pick up dry cleaning when I arrive at the mall." When you get close to the designated location, your Apple Watch will alert you.

Connecting with Family: Emergency SOS & Medical ID

The Apple Watch Series 10 is not simply a communication tool—it's also an essential safety gadget that can help you in case of crises. Two crucial elements that can make a major difference are Emergency SOS and Medical ID. These tools can help you stay safe by notifying emergency contacts and providing medical information to first responders in case of an emergency.

Using Emergency SOS

The **Emergency SOS** feature on your Apple Watch Series 10 allows you to call emergency services with just a press of a button, even if you're unable to speak or move. This can be a life-saving tool in an emergency situation.

Here's how to use Emergency SOS on your Apple Watch:

1. **Activating Emergency SOS:** To activate Emergency SOS, press and hold the **Side Button** and the **Digital Crown** simultaneously for a few seconds. You'll hear a countdown, and then the watch will automatically dial **911** (or your local emergency number). If you're unable to speak, the emergency services will receive your location and know that you need help.

2. **Alerting Emergency Contacts:** Once the emergency call is made, your Apple Watch will send an alert to your designated emergency contacts, letting them know that you're in trouble. You can set up your emergency contacts through the **Health app** on your iPhone.

3. **Stopping the Emergency Call:** If you accidentally trigger Emergency SOS, you can cancel the call by tapping **Stop** on the screen before the countdown finishes. If you miss the countdown and the call is made, simply speak to the operator and explain that it was an accident.

Setting Up Medical ID

Your **Medical ID** provides essential health information, such as allergies, medical conditions, medications, and emergency contacts, and it can be accessed by first responders directly from your Apple Watch. Here's how to set it up:

1. **Creating Your Medical ID:** Open the **Health app** on your iPhone and tap the **Medical ID** tab. Enter your name, date of birth, medical conditions, medications, allergies, and emergency contacts.

2. **Accessing Medical ID in an Emergency:** When you press the **Side Button** to trigger Emergency SOS, first responders can swipe your Apple Watch screen to access your Medical ID. This allows them to quickly gather critical information to provide the best care possible.

3. **Making Your Medical ID Public:** You can choose to make your Medical ID accessible even when your watch is locked. To enable this, go to **Settings > Health > Medical ID**, and toggle the **Show When Locked** option.

Staying connected is one of the key benefits of your Apple Watch Series 10. Whether it's managing notifications, staying on top of your emails and calendar events, or keeping your loved ones informed in case of an emergency, your watch is meant to help you stay organized and secure. With options like Emergency SOS, Medical ID, and personalized notifications, your Apple Watch is not just a piece of technology—it's a trustworthy companion that helps keep you connected to what matters most.

Chapter 5

Health and Wellness Features for Seniors

Setting Up the Health App

The Apple Watch Series 10 is not just a smartwatch—it's a personal health companion. From tracking physical activity to monitoring your heart rate and sleep habits, the watch is equipped with a variety of health-focused features designed to promote your overall well-being. One of the most significant aspects of the Apple Watch is the Health app.

The Health app functions as a central hub for all of your health data. It tracks everything from your step count and workout to your heart rate, sleep habits, and more. This chapter will lead you through setting up the Health app on your Apple Watch and show you how to use it to track your health.

What is the Health App?

The Health app is a built-in app on your Apple Watch and iPhone that helps you monitor and track a number of health parameters. The information from your watch, such as your activity levels, heart rate, and other health-related data, is kept in the Health app. This data can be evaluated over time to help you make informed decisions regarding your lifestyle and wellness.

For elders, the Health app is a wonderful tool. It gives you real-time insights into your physical activity, helps you create and achieve health objectives, and even provides alarms if it identifies unusual health patterns that could require medical care.

Setting Up the Health App

Setting up the Health app is easy, and it only takes a few steps to get started:

1. **Open the Health App on Your iPhone**
   The Health app comes pre-installed on most iPhones, so you won't need to download it. Open the **Health app** on your iPhone to begin the setup process.

2. **Set Up Your Profile**
   The first time you open the app, you'll be prompted to create a health profile. This profile will include basic information about you, such as your **age**, **height**, **weight**, and **gender**. This data will help the Health app give you more accurate readings based on your specific health profile.

3. **Allow Data to Sync from Your Apple Watch**

   If you haven't already paired your Apple Watch with your iPhone, you'll need to do so. When paired, the Apple Watch will automatically sync its data to the Health app, including your daily steps, exercise minutes, heart rate, and more.

4. **Choose What to Track**

   In the Health app, you'll have the option to select what kind of health data you'd like to track. This includes everything from **activity levels**, **nutrition**, and **sleep**, to **heart health**, **mindfulness**, and **medication reminders**. You can choose the metrics that are most important to you, and the app will provide feedback on your progress.

5. **Enable Notifications**

   The Health app can notify you when you reach certain milestones or when you've been inactive for a certain amount of time. To enable these notifications, go to the **Health app > Health Data > Activity** and turn on the **Reminders** for goal completion or inactivity.

Understanding Health Data in the App

Once your Health app is set up, you'll start seeing real-time data about your daily activities, fitness levels, and health status. The app organizes this data into clear charts and graphs, which makes it easy for you to understand how you're doing. The main sections of the Health app include:

- **Summary**: This is where you can see your overall health data for the day. It includes your **steps**, **exercise minutes**, and other important metrics like **distance traveled** and **calories burned**.

- **Health Data**: In this section, you can dig deeper into specific health categories, such as **Heart Rate**, **Sleep**, and **Blood Oxygen Levels**. Each category has a detailed breakdown of your metrics over time.

- **Mindfulness**: For mental well-being, the Health app includes data on your mindfulness sessions, such as breathing exercises and meditation.

Heart Rate Monitoring – What It Tells You

One of the most essential health features on the Apple Watch Series 10 is its heart rate tracking. Your heart rate is a critical sign of your general health, and having it routinely monitored is essential—especially as we age. The Apple Watch can offer you real-time heart rate readings throughout the day, providing you insights into your fitness levels and alerting you to any potential difficulties.

How Does the Apple Watch Measure Heart Rate?

The Apple device Series 10 uses optical cardiac sensors positioned on the rear of the device to measure your heart rate. These sensors employ green LED lights that beam onto your skin and measure the amount of light that bounces back. This method allows the watch to correctly determine the number of times your heart beats per minute, presenting you with your heart rate statistics.

Using Heart Rate Monitoring on the Apple Watch

1. **Automatic Heart Rate Monitoring**
   Your Apple Watch will automatically monitor your heart rate throughout the day. It checks your heart rate periodically and stores the data in the Health app, so you can see how your heart rate changes over time.

2. **Viewing Heart Rate Data**
   To see your current heart rate, simply open the **Heart Rate app** on your Apple Watch (it looks like a heart icon). Your current heart rate will be displayed on the screen in beats per minute (bpm). If you want to see historical data, you can check the **Health app** on your iPhone to view detailed graphs and trends over time.

3. **Understanding Your Heart Rate Zones**
   The Apple Watch also helps you understand how your heart rate compares to different **heart rate zones**. These zones are based on your age, fitness level, and health goals and include categories like **resting heart rate**, **fat-burning zone**, **cardio zone**, and **maximum heart rate**.

   o **Resting Heart Rate**: This is the number of beats per minute when you're at rest. A lower resting heart rate generally indicates better cardiovascular fitness.

   o **Fat-Burning Zone**: This is when your heart rate is elevated to a moderate level, which helps with fat burning during exercise.

   o **Cardio Zone**: This zone is where you're working out at a higher intensity, improving your cardiovascular fitness.

   o **Maximum Heart Rate**: This is the highest heart rate you can safely achieve during exercise. It's important to avoid staying in this zone for prolonged periods of time, especially as we age.

4. **Heart Rate Alerts**

   If your heart rate goes above or below a certain threshold, your Apple Watch will send you an alert. This is particularly helpful if you have a heart condition or want to monitor your heart health more closely. You can customize these thresholds in the **Health app** to match your health goals.

5. **Resting Heart Rate Trends**

   One of the most useful things your Apple Watch can do is track your **resting heart rate** over time. A rising resting heart rate can sometimes indicate an underlying health issue, so it's helpful to monitor this trend regularly. You'll be able to see if your resting heart rate increases over time, which might be a sign to speak with a healthcare provider.

ECG and Blood Oxygen – Step-by-Step Guide

The Apple Watch Series 10 takes heart health monitoring to the next level with its ability to perform an ECG (electrocardiogram) and detect blood oxygen levels. These two characteristics can provide a deep look into your cardiovascular health and overall well-being. Let's take a closer look at each of these features and how to use them.

ECG - What It Is and How to Use It

An ECG is a medical test that measures the electrical activity of your heart. It records the timing and strength of the electrical signals that initiate each heartbeat. The Apple Watch Series 10 is capable of performing an ECG directly from your wrist, providing you with real-time data on your heart's rhythm.

How to Use the ECG Feature on Your Apple Watch

1. **Set Up the ECG App**

   To use the ECG feature on your Apple Watch, make sure the **ECG app** is enabled. Open the **Apple Watch app** on your iPhone, go to **My Watch**, then tap **Health** and make sure the ECG feature is turned on.

2. **Performing an ECG**

   o Open the **ECG app** on your Apple Watch (the icon looks like an ECG waveform).

   o Place **one finger** from your opposite hand on the **Digital Crown** of your Apple Watch. This creates a circuit between your finger and the back of the watch, allowing it to measure the electrical signals from your heart.

- ○ The ECG test takes about **30 seconds** to complete. You'll see a waveform appear on the screen while the test is being conducted.

- ○ Once the test is complete, the watch will display the results, which can range from **Normal sinus rhythm** to **Atrial fibrillation (AFib)**, depending on the data it detects.

3. **Understanding Your ECG Results**
   After the test, the Apple Watch will provide a result indicating whether your heart's rhythm is normal or if there are signs of an irregular rhythm (such as AFib). AFib is a condition where the heart beats irregularly and rapidly, increasing the risk of stroke and other complications. If AFib is detected, you'll be advised to follow up with your healthcare provider.

4. **Sharing Your ECG Results**
   The ECG results can be saved to the **Health app** on your iPhone, where you can track the results over time. You can also share these results with your doctor by exporting the data in PDF format.

Blood Oxygen – What It Is and How to Use It

Blood oxygen levels (SpO2) are a critical measure of how well oxygen is being transported throughout your body. Low oxygen levels can indicate respiratory issues or other health problems, making this feature on the Apple Watch a valuable tool for staying on top of your health.

How to Measure Blood Oxygen on Your Apple Watch

1. **Open the Blood Oxygen App**
   The **Blood Oxygen app** on your Apple Watch is where you can measure your oxygen levels. To use it, press the **Digital Crown** to open the Home Screen and tap on the **Blood Oxygen app**.

2. **Positioning Your Watch**
   For the best accuracy, make sure your Apple Watch is snug on your wrist and that your arm is resting comfortably on a flat surface. Hold your wrist still for about 15 seconds during the measurement.

3. **Starting the Measurement**
   Once your wrist is still, tap **Start** on the Blood Oxygen app, and the watch will begin

measuring your oxygen levels. The measurement typically takes about **15 seconds** to complete. During this time, the Apple Watch will use its infrared sensors to check the color of your blood and calculate the amount of oxygen present.

4. **Viewing the Results**

   After the measurement is complete, the app will display your **blood oxygen percentage**, which typically ranges between **95% and 100%** for healthy individuals. Anything below 90% would indicate a potential issue with your respiratory or cardiovascular health, and you should consult your healthcare provider.

5. **Tracking Blood Oxygen Levels Over Time**

   Your blood oxygen readings are automatically recorded and stored in the **Health app** on your iPhone. You can review your levels over time to spot any trends or changes that might indicate health concerns.

The Apple Watch Series 10 offers seniors a wealth of features to track and monitor their health, including heart rate monitoring, ECG, and blood oxygen levels. These tools give you real-time insights about your heart health and overall wellness, helping you stay informed and take action when necessary. Whether you're checking your heart rate, performing an ECG, or analyzing your blood oxygen levels, the Apple Watch becomes a useful partner in managing your health.

Fall Detection: How It Works & Why It Matters

As we age, the chance of falling increases, and the consequences of a fall might be significantly more serious. Whether due to a health condition, frailty, or just a sudden slip of balance, falls can lead to major injuries or even death. The good news is that the Apple Watch Series 10 contains a Fall Detection feature that might be a life-saver in such instances.

What Is Fall Detection?

Fall Detection is a built-in feature of the Apple Watch Series 10 that can identify when you have fallen. It uses a mix of accelerometer and gyroscope sensors to measure the motion and direction of your wrist. When it detects an abrupt movement that indicates a fall, the watch will immediately launch a series of procedures to help you receive assistance.

If the watch senses a fall, it initially waits for a few moments to check if you get back up. If you do, it assumes that no assistance is needed. If you remain motionless after a fall, however, the watch will prompt you with an alert on the screen asking if you are okay. This popup will give you the option to call emergency services or reject the warning.

How Does Fall Detection Work?

1. **Detection**
   The Apple Watch uses sensors to detect a sudden change in movement. For instance, if you were standing and suddenly lost your balance, the watch would register the abrupt motion as a fall.

2. **Alerting the User**
   If you remain immobile for about 30 seconds after the fall, the watch will send you a **haptic alert** (a small vibration on your wrist), followed by an on-screen notification asking if you're okay.

3. **Emergency SOS Activation**
   If you do not respond to the fall detection prompt, the Apple Watch will automatically initiate the **Emergency SOS** feature. This means it will automatically call **911** or the local emergency services number, and alert your **emergency contacts** that you have fallen and may need help.

4. **Important Considerations**

   o **Sensitivity**: Fall Detection is designed to detect hard falls, so it may not always register more subtle falls, such as slipping or stumbling. It's important to understand that it's a safeguard, but not a guarantee that it will detect every fall.

   o **Deactivation**: You can disable Fall Detection if you prefer not to use this feature. This can be done from the **Settings app** on your Apple Watch or in the **Apple Watch app** on your iPhone. However, for most seniors, it's highly recommended to leave Fall Detection enabled for peace of mind.

Why Fall Detection Matters for Seniors

Falls can happen at any time, and for seniors, the consequences can be catastrophic. According to the Centers for Disease Control and Prevention (CDC), one out of four older persons falls each year. Falls are a primary cause of injury-related death among seniors, and they often lead to fractures, head injuries, and long recovery times.

The Fall Detection feature on your Apple Watch provides a safety net, guaranteeing that in the case of a fall, help is only a few seconds away. It offers reassurance, especially for seniors who live alone or spend a large amount of time without fast access to support.

Activity Rings: Staying Active Safely

The Apple Watch Series 10 encourages healthy living through its Activity Rings, a feature meant to help you measure and improve your daily activity. Staying physically active is one of the best ways to preserve your health, prevent chronic diseases, and feel better overall. The Activity Rings give a fun and visible method to track your movement, exercise, and standing activity throughout the day.

What Are Activity Rings?

The Activity Rings are three **visual indicators** on the Apple Watch that track your daily physical activity. The rings represent:

1. **Move (Red Ring)**: The Move ring shows how many active calories you've burned throughout the day. You set a **Move goal** when you first set up the watch, and the goal is represented by the red ring. The goal can be customized based on your fitness level and daily routine.

2. **Exercise (Green Ring)**: The Exercise ring tracks the amount of time you've spent doing **moderate-to-intense physical activity**. Aiming for at least **30 minutes of exercise** each day is recommended for general health, and the green ring will fill as you complete each session of activity.

3. **Stand (Blue Ring)**: The Stand ring tracks how many hours during the day you've stood up for at least one minute. The goal is to encourage you to get up and move every hour, reducing the risk of a sedentary lifestyle that can be harmful to your health.

How to Use Activity Rings to Stay Active

The Activity Rings provide a simple, motivating visual to track your daily activity. Here's how you can use them to stay on track with your health goals:

1. **Set Your Goals**
   The first step in using the Activity Rings is setting personal goals for each of the three categories: Move, Exercise, and Stand. These goals are adjustable and can be modified based on your activity levels, personal preferences, and health conditions. If you're starting out with a low level of activity, you might want to start with a modest Move goal and gradually increase it as you improve.

2. **Track Your Progress**
   As you go through your day, your Apple Watch will continuously track your activity, and

you can check your progress by glancing at the **Activity app** on your watch. Each ring will fill up as you complete the activity:

- The **red Move ring** will fill as you burn active calories through exercise or daily movement.

- The **green Exercise ring** will fill based on your duration of moderate or vigorous activity.

- The **blue Stand ring** will fill when you stand for one minute in each hour.

3. **Notifications and Reminders**
   The Apple Watch will send you reminders throughout the day to help you stay on track. If you haven't stood up within an hour, you'll get a gentle reminder to get up and move. Similarly, if you're close to completing your Move or Exercise goal, you'll receive a notification encouraging you to finish the task.

4. **Activity Sharing and Motivation**
   You can share your Activity progress with friends or family members who also use an Apple Watch. This can be a great source of **motivation**, as you can cheer each other on, set group goals, and even compete in activity challenges.

Why Activity Rings Matter for Seniors

For seniors, being active is vital for maintaining mobility, strength, and independence. According to the American Heart Association, older persons who engage in regular physical activity have a lower risk of heart disease, stroke, diabetes, and other chronic illnesses. Regular exercise also helps to improve mood, enhance cognitive function, and minimize the risk of falls.

By using the Activity Rings, seniors can maintain their physical health in a fun and stimulating way. The rings visibly illustrate progress and encourage a balanced approach to staying active throughout the day, helping to avoid the hazards of a sedentary lifestyle.

Sleep Tracking for Better Rest

Getting adequate restful sleep is vital for overall health, and the Apple Watch Series 10 offers strong sleep-tracking functions that allow you to monitor and improve your sleep habits. Sleep is crucial for physical healing, mental clarity, and emotional well-being, yet many people—especially seniors—struggle to get enough quality sleep.

How Does Sleep Tracking Work?

The Apple Watch Series 10 uses enhanced motion sensors and heart rate tracking to track your sleep. While you wear the watch overnight, it automatically identifies when you fall asleep and when you wake up, delivering a thorough picture of your sleep habits. It doesn't require any user input, making it an easy tool for monitoring your sleep without effort.

Setting Up Sleep Tracking

To get started with sleep tracking, follow these steps:

1. **Open the Health App on Your iPhone**
   The Health app on your iPhone is where you'll find all your sleep data. Make sure that **Sleep** is enabled in the **Health app** by going to the **Browse** tab and selecting **Sleep**.

2. **Set Up Sleep Goals**
   In the Health app, you can set your sleep goal. Most adults need about **7-9 hours of sleep** per night, but this can vary based on individual needs. You can adjust your goal based on how much sleep you feel you need to feel rested.

3. **Sleep Mode on Your Apple Watch**
   To track your sleep, your Apple Watch needs to be worn while you sleep. The watch will automatically enter **Sleep Mode** when you go to bed. Sleep Mode helps reduce distractions by dimming the screen and muting notifications.

4. **Reviewing Your Sleep Data**
   After you wake up, you can review your sleep data in the **Health app** on your iPhone. The app will show you how long you slept, how much time you spent in different stages of sleep (such as light or deep sleep), and the consistency of your sleep schedule.

Why Sleep Tracking Matters for Seniors

As we age, sleep patterns often change. Seniors may experience difficulty falling asleep, staying asleep, or achieving restorative sleep. According to the **National Sleep Foundation**, sleep issues in older adults are common and can affect overall health, including cognitive function, mood, and immune system strength.

By using **sleep tracking**, seniors can gain valuable insights into their sleep patterns. It can help you identify issues such as:

- Poor sleep quality or insufficient sleep duration.

- Late bedtimes or inconsistent sleep schedules.

- Interrupted sleep patterns that could indicate health concerns.

Tracking your sleep can motivate you to make healthier changes, like adjusting your bedtime, improving your sleep environment, or consulting with a healthcare provider about sleep-related issues.

Mindfulness and Breathing Exercises

In addition to physical activity, mental well-being is just as vital for elders. The Apple Watch Series 10 features Mindfulness and Breathing exercises that can help you stay calm, focused, and emotionally balanced. These methods are designed to relieve stress, increase mental clarity, and promote a sense of overall well-being.

How to Use Mindfulness on Your Apple Watch

The **Mindfulness app** helps you take short breaks during the day to focus on your breathing and relieve stress. This app offers two key features: **Breathe** and **Reflect**.

1. **Breathe**
   The **Breathe app** guides you through a series of deep breathing exercises that can help lower stress and anxiety. To use the Breathe app:

   - Open the **Mindfulness app** on your Apple Watch.

   - Tap **Breathe** and select a session length (1, 3, or 5 minutes).

   - The watch will guide you through deep breaths, using gentle haptic feedback and a visual guide to help you inhale and exhale slowly.

2. Research shows that regular deep breathing can improve heart health, reduce stress levels, and even improve sleep quality.

3. **Reflect**
   The **Reflect** feature encourages you to take a moment to think about something positive in your life. You can use it to focus on a specific intention or mindfulness topic. The watch will provide a prompt, such as "Think about something that makes you happy" or

"Reflect on a challenge you overcame." This quick practice helps foster gratitude and mental clarity, making it an excellent tool for promoting emotional well-being.

Why Mindfulness Matters for Seniors

Mindfulness techniques, including deep breathing and reflection, can have considerable advantages for elders. Reducing stress helps improve heart health, reduce blood pressure, and even enhance cognitive performance. Taking little breaks throughout the day to focus on your breath can make a tremendous impact in how you feel emotionally and mentally.

The Apple Watch Series 10 is much more than just a smartwatch; it's a health and wellness companion that empowers you to monitor and enhance your physical and mental health. Features like Fall Detection, Activity Rings, Sleep Tracking, and Mindfulness exercises work together to provide you a comprehensive approach to wellness, helping you stay active, balanced, and connected.

By making use of these health features, seniors may live healthier, more satisfying lives, with the support of their Apple Watch every step of the way. Whether it's tracking your physical activity, enhancing your sleep, or managing stress, the Apple Watch is there to help you stay in control of your health.

Chapter 6

Fitness and Exercise with Apple Watch

As we age, remaining physically active becomes more crucial than ever. Regular exercise improves heart health, promotes mobility, elevates happiness, and enhances cognitive function. However, many seniors experience difficulty when it comes to keeping a consistent fitness routine. Whether it's due to physical constraints or simply a lack of motivation, the need for an accessible and dependable approach to track and improve fitness is vital.

That's where the Apple Watch Series 10 comes in. More than simply a gorgeous accessory, the Apple Watch is a strong fitness and health companion that helps you stay active and involved in your wellness path. With features like the Workout app, step tracking, and configurable fitness objectives, your Apple Watch makes it easier to monitor your activity, establish reasonable goals, and measure your progress over time.

In this chapter, we'll explore how to use the Apple Watch to boost your workout regimen. Whether you're walking, jogging, cycling, or doing any other sort of activity, the Apple Watch Series 10 offers you with the tools and data to stay motivated and healthy.

Using the Workout App

The Workout app on the Apple Watch is your primary tool for tracking physical activity. Whether you're strolling around the block, performing yoga, or indulging in more rigorous workouts, the app allows you to track your heart rate, calories burned, and other critical parameters.

Getting Started with the Workout App

When you first start the Workout app on your Apple Watch, you'll see a list of different workout kinds you may choose from. These include walking, jogging, swimming, cycling, and more. The software is incredibly versatile and may be adjusted based on your fitness preferences.

How to Start a Workout:

1. **Open the Workout App**
   Press the **Digital Crown** to go to the Home Screen, then tap the **Workout app** (it looks like a running figure).

2. **Select a Workout Type**
   Scroll through the list of workout options. Some of the available workouts include:

   - ○ **Outdoor Walk**: Perfect for seniors who want to track their steps and distance while walking outside.

   - ○ **Indoor Walk**: For walking on a treadmill or any indoor space.

   - ○ **Outdoor Run**: A great option for those who enjoy running.

   - ○ **Cycling**: Tracks your cycling distance, speed, and calories.

   - ○ **Swimming**: If you enjoy swimming, the Apple Watch Series 10 is **water-resistant** and can track your swim metrics.

   - ○ **Yoga**: For gentle, mind-body exercises like yoga.

   - ○ **Strength Training**: For weightlifting and resistance exercises.

3. **Tap to Start**
   After choosing your workout, tap the **Start** button. Your Apple Watch will begin tracking your workout data, including your **heart rate**, **calories burned**, **distance**, and **duration**.

During Your Workout:

Once your workout has started, the Apple Watch will display real-time data on the screen. You'll see your **heart rate**, the **time elapsed**, **calories burned**, and **distance** covered (if applicable). You can interact with the screen to toggle between different views and focus on the data that matters most to you.

- **Heart Rate Monitoring**: Your Apple Watch continuously monitors your heart rate during your workout. It will show you your **current heart rate** in real-time, and you can track whether you're in the **fat-burning zone**, **cardio zone**, or other heart rate zones.

- **Pace and Speed**: For workouts like running and cycling, the watch will track your pace and speed. This is especially helpful if you want to track improvements or maintain a steady pace.

- **Calories Burned**: The app will also estimate how many **active calories** you've burned during your workout. This is valuable for tracking weight loss or fitness progress over time.

Ending Your Workout:

When you've completed your workout, tap the **End** button to finish tracking. You'll then be shown a summary of your workout stats, including:

- **Total duration**

- **Calories burned**

- **Average heart rate**

- **Distance covered (if applicable)**

Your workout data is automatically saved in the **Health app** on your iPhone, so you can review your progress over time and see how you're improving.

Tracking Steps, Distance, and Calories

Three of the most significant variables for tracking your physical activity are steps, distance, and calories. The Apple Watch Series 10 tracks these parameters throughout the day, letting you keep aware of your activity levels and make adjustments to your fitness program.

Tracking Steps:

Your Apple Watch records the amount of steps you walk each day using its built-in accelerometer. This function is particularly valuable for seniors who are trying to stay active but may not have the ability to engage in high-intensity activities. Walking is a low-impact exercise that can have considerable health advantages, and the Apple Watch makes it easy to measure your progress.

How to Track Your Steps:

- **Activity App**: The **Activity app** on your Apple Watch shows your **daily step count**. The **Move ring** represents your daily activity goal, while the **Stand ring** shows how often you've stood up during the day.

- **Health App**: All your step data is also synced with the **Health app** on your iPhone, where you can view detailed stats and trends. You can check how many steps you've taken each day, week, or month and track your overall activity levels over time.

Tracking Distance:

For those who enjoy walking, running, or cycling, tracking your **distance** can be a great way to monitor progress and set fitness goals. The Apple Watch Series 10 uses **GPS** (on the cellular model) or your iPhone's GPS (on the GPS-only model) to track your distance during outdoor workouts.

How to Track Your Distance:

- **Outdoor Walk/Run/Cycle**: When you start a workout, your Apple Watch will automatically begin tracking your **distance**. If you're walking outdoors, it will measure the distance you cover in real time and display it on your watch face.

- **Indoor Workouts**: If you're indoors, such as on a treadmill or stationary bike, the Apple Watch uses **calibration** to estimate your distance based on your steps and activity.

Tracking Calories:

The Apple Watch calculates the **active calories** you burn throughout the day based on your activity level. Active calories are those burned through intentional exercise and movement. The more you move, the more calories you burn, and your Apple Watch helps you stay motivated by showing you how much progress you've made toward your **Move goal**.

How to Track Calories:

- **Move Ring**: The **red Move ring** is the primary way the Apple Watch tracks calories. It shows you how many active calories you've burned throughout the day, with a goal you can customize.

- **Workout App**: During your workout, your Apple Watch tracks how many calories you burn based on the intensity of your activity. After the workout, you can see a detailed breakdown of your **total calories burned** and **active calories**.

Customizing Exercise Goals

One of the most powerful aspects of the Apple Watch is its ability to customize your activity goals. Setting realistic, specific objectives can keep you motivated and help you stay on track with your workout program.

Why Customizing Exercise Goals Matters

As we age, it's crucial to alter fitness goals to match our specific needs. For seniors, creating reasonable and safe goals will help you keep active without overexerting yourself. Whether your objective is to walk more steps, burn more calories, or simply get up more frequently, the Apple Watch lets you customize the Move, Exercise, and Stand goals to suit your lifestyle.

How to Customize Your Goals:

1. **Changing the Move Goal**
   The **Move goal** represents the number of active calories you want to burn each day. To adjust your Move goal:

   - Open the **Activity app** on your Apple Watch.

   - Press and hold the **Move ring**.

   - Tap the **Change Move Goal** option.

   - Use the + and - buttons to adjust your calorie goal.

2. **Changing the Exercise Goal**
   The **Exercise goal** is a measure of how much time you spend engaging in moderate-to-vigorous activity each day. The default goal is 30 minutes of exercise per day, but you can adjust this to a lower or higher number based on your preferences.

   - To change the Exercise goal, go to the **Activity app**, press and hold the **Exercise ring**, and adjust the goal by tapping **Change Exercise Goal**.

3. **Changing the Stand Goal**
   The **Stand goal** encourages you to stand for at least one minute in each hour throughout the day. You can adjust this goal based on your personal preferences, but the default is usually set to **12 hours**.

- To change the Stand goal, open the **Activity app**, press and hold the **Stand ring**, and adjust it by selecting **Change Stand Goal**.

Staying Motivated with Personalized Goals

When you set personalized fitness goals, you can increase your chances of sticking with them. The Apple Watch Series 10 helps you track your progress and provides **gentle reminders** throughout the day to keep you on track. Whether you're working toward a higher calorie goal or aiming for more minutes of exercise, the watch offers **real-time feedback** and keeps you motivated.

Outdoor vs. Indoor Workouts

Staying physically active is vital at every stage of life, and the Apple Watch Series 10 includes a number of capabilities to help you remain on track with your fitness objectives. Whether you prefer the fresh air of outdoor fitness or the controlled environment of indoor exercises, your Apple Watch has the capabilities to accompany you in both scenarios.

Outdoor Workouts: Benefits and Features

Outdoor workouts give special benefits, particularly for seniors. Exercising outside exposes you to fresh air, sunlight, and various terrain, which can improve your physical and emotional well-being. Additionally, outdoor activities like walking, running, or cycling give a fantastic chance to appreciate nature while being fit.

How Apple Watch Tracks Outdoor Workouts:

The Apple Watch Series 10 uses a combination of built-in GPS and heart rate sensors to properly track your outdoor workouts. Here are some of the important outdoor exercises that the watch can monitor:

1. **Outdoor Walk**: This is one of the most accessible and low-impact forms of exercise, making it ideal for seniors. The Apple Watch tracks your steps, distance, heart rate, and calories burned, providing real-time feedback as you walk. If you're walking outdoors, the watch uses GPS to track your route, helping you see your distance and pace.

2. **Outdoor Run**: If you enjoy running, the Apple Watch can track your distance, pace, heart rate, and calories burned during outdoor runs. GPS provides precise data about your route and speed, while the watch monitors your heart rate to help ensure that you're in a healthy zone for your fitness level.

3. **Cycling**: Whether you're cycling on the road or on a trail, the Apple Watch tracks your distance, speed, and heart rate. The watch uses GPS to record your route and provides feedback on your pace and the number of calories burned during the ride.

4. **Hiking**: If you prefer hiking, Apple Watch can track your altitude, route, and heart rate during your trek, making it a great tool for monitoring your physical activity in natural environments.

5. **Swimming (Outdoor Pools)**: For seniors who enjoy swimming in outdoor pools, the Apple Watch Series 10 provides accurate tracking of laps, distance, and stroke type. The watch is water-resistant, so you can comfortably wear it while swimming.

Benefits of Outdoor Workouts:

- **Exposure to Vitamin D**: Sunlight helps your body produce vitamin D, which is essential for bone health and immune function. Outdoor workouts, especially in the morning, can provide a natural source of vitamin D.

- **Mental Health Benefits**: Studies have shown that outdoor exercise, particularly in green spaces, helps reduce stress, anxiety, and depression. The changing scenery can provide mental stimulation and improve mood.

- **Varied Terrain**: Exercising on different types of terrain—whether it's a walking trail, a park, or an outdoor track—engages more muscles and improves balance and coordination.

Outdoor Workouts on Apple Watch:

To begin an outdoor workout, press the **Digital Crown** to open the Home Screen, tap on the **Workout app,** and choose the **Outdoor Walk, Outdoor Run, Cycling,** or **Hiking** option. When you start the workout, your Apple Watch will automatically activate GPS and heart rate monitoring.

The Apple Watch will show you real-time data, including:

- **Time elapsed**

- **Distance traveled**

- **Pace or speed**

- **Heart rate**

- **Calories burned**

As you progress in your workout, the watch will provide updates, motivating you to reach your goals. After completing the workout, you'll receive a summary of the metrics, and this data will sync to the **Health app** for further analysis.

Indoor Workouts: Convenience and Control

While outdoor workouts bring excellent benefits, indoor workouts have their own perks. For many seniors, indoor exercises offer a more controlled setting, where the weather, terrain, and external influences are less of a worry. Indoor exercise choices like walking on a treadmill, using a stationary bike, or doing yoga give consistent and reasonable settings for staying healthy.

How Apple Watch Tracks Indoor Workouts:

1. **Indoor Walk**: For seniors who prefer walking indoors, the Apple Watch tracks your movement on a treadmill or any flat surface. The watch measures your steps, heart rate, and calories burned, and it uses the **accelerometer** to detect movement. It doesn't require GPS because it's tracking your movement indoors.

2. **Indoor Run**: If you enjoy running on a treadmill, the Apple Watch can monitor your heart rate, distance, speed, and calories burned. It can even track your pace to help you set goals and improve your performance over time.

3. **Stationary Cycling**: Using a stationary bike? The Apple Watch can track the time, heart rate, calories burned, and the intensity of your workout, so you can stay on track with your fitness goals. If you're using a bike with a built-in tracking system, the watch can integrate data to ensure accurate measurements.

4. **Strength Training**: Strength exercises are essential for seniors, helping to build muscle mass and improve bone density. The Apple Watch can track your weightlifting sessions, including the number of sets and reps, as well as the duration of your workout.

5. **Yoga**: Indoor yoga sessions are perfect for improving flexibility, balance, and mental well-being. The Apple Watch can monitor your heart rate during yoga, helping you stay within a healthy range while focusing on breathing and posture.

6. **Swimming (Indoor Pools)**: If you're swimming in an indoor pool, the Apple Watch can track your laps, distance, and stroke type, just like it does for outdoor pools. The watch is water-resistant and designed for use in pools, making it a great option for seniors who enjoy aquatic exercise.

Benefits of Indoor Workouts:

- **Controlled Environment**: You're not affected by external weather conditions or terrain. Whether it's raining outside or too hot to go for a walk, indoor workouts offer a stable environment for exercise.

- **Customizable Intensity**: Indoor workouts allow you to control the intensity of your exercises. On a treadmill or stationary bike, you can easily adjust the speed and resistance to match your fitness level.

- **Accessibility**: For seniors with mobility issues or other physical concerns, indoor workouts like seated exercises or yoga can be tailored to suit personal needs.

Indoor Workouts on Apple Watch:

To begin an indoor workout, open the **Workout app** on your Apple Watch, then select the appropriate indoor activity, such as **Indoor Walk, Indoor Run, Stationary Bike, Strength Training**, or **Yoga**. The watch will track your exercise using sensors like the **accelerometer** and **heart rate monitor**.

During the workout, you'll see your **duration**, **heart rate**, **calories burned**, and **steps** in real-time. Once you complete the workout, the summary will be displayed on your watch, and the data will be recorded in the **Health app** on your iPhone.

Sharing Progress with Friends and Family

One of the most motivating components of fitness is having support from friends and family. With the Apple Watch Series 10, sharing your fitness progress with others has never been easier. By allowing friends or family members to follow your workouts and activity, you generate a sense of accountability and support that can help you stay on track.

How to Share Your Activity with Others

The **Activity app** on the Apple Watch allows you to share your progress with others who are also using the Apple Watch. You can create a **Sharing** group where you and your friends or family can compete in friendly challenges or simply motivate each other.

1. **Opening the Activity App**
   On your Apple Watch, open the **Activity app** and tap on the **Sharing** tab. This is where you can invite others to share their activity progress with you.

2. **Invite Friends and Family**
   Tap **Invite** to add friends or family members from your contact list. You'll be able to view their progress, and they can see yours. You can compare your **Activity Rings**, set goals together, and cheer each other on.

3. **Activity Competitions**
   If you're looking for a bit of friendly competition, the **Activity app** allows you to compete in weekly challenges. You can challenge others to complete a certain number of **Move** or **Exercise** goals over a seven-day period. This feature is an excellent way to stay motivated and have fun while reaching your fitness targets.

4. **Sending Encouragement**
   The Apple Watch allows you to send **cheers** or **compete in challenges** to encourage others. You can offer a simple tap or message of support to let someone know you're rooting for them. This adds a personal, social element to fitness tracking.

Why Sharing Progress Matters for Seniors

Sharing your fitness progress with others can help you stay motivated and make exercise more enjoyable. It's also a great way to stay connected with loved ones and create healthy competition. For seniors, having a support network can be incredibly motivating, helping to build consistency and routine.

Understanding Fitness Trends and Rewards

The Apple Watch Series 10 not only tracks your daily activity but also provides **detailed fitness trends** and **rewards** that can help you stay motivated to reach your fitness goals.

Fitness Trends

The **Fitness Trends** feature shows your progress over time. It tracks your **weekly** and **monthly trends**, including how many calories you've burned, your exercise minutes, and your steps. These trends give you a long-term view of your activity levels, helping you see improvements and identify areas where you might need to increase effort.

How to View Fitness Trends:

1. Open the **Activity app** on your iPhone.

2. Tap on the **Trends** tab to see an overview of your activity trends over the last month.

3. You'll be able to compare your progress from week to week or month to month, giving you a sense of accomplishment and motivation.

Fitness Rewards

Apple Watch also offers **rewards** for achieving fitness milestones. These rewards are designed to celebrate your efforts and keep you motivated.

Types of Fitness Rewards:

- **Achievement Badges**: As you hit milestones—such as completing 10,000 steps in a day or exercising for a certain number of minutes—you'll receive achievement badges. These badges are visible in your Activity app and serve as a reminder of your progress.

- **Streaks**: The Apple Watch encourages consistency by rewarding you for completing **multiple days in a row** of meeting your fitness goals. This could include completing your Move, Exercise, or Stand rings for several consecutive days.

Why Fitness Trends and Rewards Matter for Seniors

Tracking trends and receiving rewards can provide a sense of accomplishment, which is essential for maintaining motivation, especially as we age. By viewing your progress over time and celebrating small victories, you can stay engaged and committed to your fitness routine.

The Apple Watch Series 10 is a fantastic tool for seniors who want to keep active and improve their health. With features like the Workout app, Activity Rings, and the ability to track steps, distance, and calories, the Apple Watch makes it easier than ever to keep on top of your fitness objectives. Sharing progress with friends and family and understanding your fitness trends and rewards provide the support and encouragement you need to be consistent.

Chapter 7

Personalizing Your Apple Watch

The Apple Watch Series 10 is a powerful tool that helps you remain connected, measure your health, and manage your exercise goals. But what sets the Apple Watch unique from rival smartwatches is its potential to be highly customized to meet your style, preferences, and needs. Whether you're using it for fitness tracking, receiving notifications, or simply appreciating its look, personalizing your Apple Watch is a vital step toward making it your own.

In this chapter, we'll explore how you may personalize your Apple Watch to make it more functional and expressive. From changing watch faces to altering the bands, and even setting up photographs and Memoji, we'll cover everything you need to know to customize your watch in a way that enhances both its appearance and performance.

Changing Watch Faces and Styles

One of the most enjoyable and unique parts of the Apple Watch is its ability to alter the watch face to meet your style or needs. The watch face is the first thing you see when you raise your wrist, so customizing it to suit your personality or your day's agenda can help make your Apple Watch even more important.

What Are Watch Faces?

Watch faces are the display styles of your Apple Watch. They show the time, date, and other information like your heart rate, calendar events, weather updates, and more. The Apple Watch Series 10 provides a number of faces, from conventional analog designs to more modern, configurable layouts that may display a wide range of information.

How to Change Your Watch Face

Changing your watch face is simple and allows you to select from pre-installed options or create a custom one. Here's how you can do it:

1. **Open Your Watch Face**
   Begin by pressing the **Digital Crown** to open the Home Screen on your Apple Watch.

2. **Press and Hold the Watch Face**

   On your watch's Home Screen, press and hold the current watch face until the **Watch Face Selection screen** appears. This screen will allow you to browse through various faces and select a new one.

3. **Swipe to Browse Faces**

   You can swipe left or right to see different watch face styles. The Apple Watch comes with several default faces, including:

   - **Modular**: A customizable face that allows you to add multiple complications.

   - **Infographic**: A vibrant face that shows detailed data like weather, activity rings, and more.

   - **California**: A more classic, elegant watch face with traditional Roman or Arabic numerals.

   - **Simple**: A minimalist face for those who prefer a clean, uncluttered design.

4. If you want to see more faces, swipe to the end of the available options and tap on **Face Gallery** to access additional styles from the **Apple Watch app** on your iPhone.

5. **Select and Customize**

   Once you've selected a watch face, tap **Customize** to adjust its appearance. You can change the **color**, **complications**, and the **style** of the watch face to fit your needs.

6. **Complications**

   Complications are small widgets on your watch face that show additional information, like weather, calendar events, or heart rate. You can select which complications to display based on what you find most useful throughout the day.

7. **Set Your Watch Face**

   After customizing, press the **Digital Crown** to save your new watch face. You can always change it again later, or create multiple custom faces for different occasions.

Types of Watch Faces for Seniors

For seniors, choosing a watch face that displays important information clearly is essential. Here are some tips for picking the right one:

- **Larger Text**: If you have difficulty reading small text, select a watch face with larger numbers or a simple layout. Faces like **Modular** or **Simple** let you focus on just the time and other key details.

- **Activity Tracking**: If you want to monitor your health and fitness throughout the day, faces like **Activity** or **Infograph** display your exercise and movement data alongside the time.

- **Health Features**: For seniors who are managing specific health conditions, the **California** or **Utility** watch face offers a clean, easy-to-read layout, while also allowing you to add complications for heart rate or medication reminders.

Switching and Adjusting Bands

Apple Watch bands come in a broad selection of materials, styles, and sizes, allowing you to change the look and feel of your watch at any moment. Whether you're searching for a more formal appearance, a sporty style for exercising, or a comfy, breathable band for regular wear, there's an Apple Watch band for every occasion.

How to Switch Bands on Your Apple Watch

One of the most convenient features of the Apple Watch is its **easy-to-remove bands**. You can change your band quickly to fit your mood, outfit, or activity. Here's how to do it:

1. **Place the Watch on a Soft Surface**
   Lay your Apple Watch face-down on a soft surface, like a clean cloth or towel, to prevent scratches or damage while removing the band.

2. **Unlock the Band**
   On the back of the Apple Watch, you'll see two small **buttons** next to the band connectors. Press and hold one of the buttons to release the band from its slot.

3. **Remove the Band**
   While holding the button, slide the band out of the slot. Once removed, repeat the process on the other side of the watch to take off the second band piece.

4. **Insert the New Band**
   To add a new band, simply slide the new band into the slot and ensure it clicks into place. You should feel a **secure click** when the band is properly installed.

5. **Adjust the Fit**

   Most bands, such as the **Sport Band** and **Solo Loop**, can be adjusted for comfort. If you're using a **Metal Link Bracelet** or **Milanese Loop**, you can adjust the length by using the adjustment links or the magnetic clasp.

Choosing the Right Band for Seniors

As a senior, comfort and ease of use are essential when selecting a watch band. Here are some tips:

- **Comfortable Fit**: Choose a band that fits snugly but isn't too tight. Bands like the **Sport Loop** and **Solo Loop** are made from soft, flexible materials that are comfortable for all-day wear.

- **Easy to Adjust**: Look for bands that are easy to put on and remove, such as **Magnetic Milanese Loop** or **Velcro Sport Loop**. These bands can be adjusted without the need for precise measurements or tools.

- **Breathability**: If you tend to sweat or live in a hot climate, breathable bands like the **Sport Band** made of fluoroelastomer or the **Sport Loop** made of woven nylon are ideal for keeping your wrist cool and dry.

- **Fashionable Styles**: For special occasions, you may want to wear a band that matches your outfit. Options like the **Leather Band** or **Stainless Steel Link Bracelet** can give your Apple Watch a more formal or polished look.

Setting Up Photos, Albums, and Emoji

Apple Watch allows you to lend a personal touch to your device by adding your favorite photos and creating Emoji. Whether you want to showcase family photos or express yourself with a fun, animated avatar, your Apple Watch may be customized to fit your personality and hobbies.

Setting Up Photos on Your Apple Watch

One of the great ways to personalize your Apple Watch is by showing your favorite images. Apple Watch Series 10 allows you to sync chosen images from your iPhone and display them straight on your watch face or in your photo album.

How to Sync Photos to Your Apple Watch:

1. **Open the Photos App on Your iPhone**
   Begin by opening the **Photos app** on your iPhone. Select the album or specific photos you want to display on your Apple Watch.

2. **Create a Photo Album**
   If you prefer to display a specific set of images, you can create a **dedicated album**. Go to **Albums**, tap the + button, and select the photos you want to include in your new album.

3. **Sync the Album with Apple Watch**
   Once your photos are organized, open the **Apple Watch app** on your iPhone. Under **My Watch**, tap **Photos**, and choose which albums to sync with your Apple Watch. You can sync a specific number of photos (e.g., 100 photos) to ensure your watch's storage isn't overwhelmed.

4. **Display Photos on Your Watch Face**
   You can set your Apple Watch's **watch face** to display a photo from the album. To do this, press and hold the current watch face on your Apple Watch, then select **Customize**. Scroll to the **Photo Watch Face**, and choose the album you'd like to display.

Why Photos Matter for Personalization:

Displaying personal photos on your watch face allows you to carry memories with you throughout the day. Whether it's pictures of family, pets, or favorite places, your watch becomes a canvas for your most cherished memories.

Creating and Using Emoji on Apple Watch

Another fun way to personalize your Apple Watch is by creating an Emoji. Emoji are animated, customizable avatars that can be used in messages, notifications, and even on your watch face. You can create an Emoji that looks like you, or experiment with fun features to express your mood or personality.

How to Create a Emoji:

1. **Open the Messages App**
   Open the **Messages app** on your iPhone and start a new conversation or open an existing one.

2. **Tap the Emoji Icon**

   In the **Messages app**, tap the **Memoji icon** (the face with a crown). This will bring up the **Memoji editor**.

3. **Customize Your Emoji**

   The Memoji editor lets you create a personalized avatar. Choose skin tone, hairstyle, eye shape, clothing, and accessories to make the Emoji look just like you. You can even change facial expressions, such as smiling, winking, or sticking out your tongue.

4. **Use Emoji in Messages**

   Once your Memoji is created, you can use it in the **Messages app** or **FaceTime** to make conversations more engaging. You can send your Memoji as an animated sticker or even record an animated Memoji video that mimics your facial expressions.

5. **Display Emoji on Your Watch Face**

   To use an Emoji on your watch face, go to the **Apple Watch app** on your iPhone and select **Watch Face Gallery**. Choose the **Memoji** face style and customize it by selecting your desired Emoji.

Why Memoji Add Fun to Your Watch:

Memoji bring a lighthearted touch to your Apple Watch experience. They allow you to express yourself visually, whether it's a quirky animated avatar that reflects your mood or a fun way to share personalized stickers in messages.

Personalizing your Apple Watch Series 10 is one of the best ways to make the device truly yours. Whether you're changing watch faces to match your mood, altering bands for comfort or design, or adding photographs and Emoji for personal flair, your Apple Watch can change to meet your lifestyle.

Adjusting Sounds, Haptics, and Brightness

The Apple Watch Series 10 comes loaded with a range of settings that allow you to alter how the watch interacts with you—particularly when it comes to audio, haptics, and brightness. These changes are critical for seniors who may have special demands involving hearing, tactile feedback, and visibility.

Adjusting Sound and Volume

The Apple Watch gives you full control over its sound settings, ensuring you can adjust it to suit your hearing preferences. Whether you want a louder or quieter alert, the watch offers an intuitive way to change the sound and volume.

1. **Setting the Volume**
    To adjust the volume of your Apple Watch, go to the **Settings app** on your watch, then tap **Sounds & Haptics**. From here, you can use the slider to increase or decrease the volume. This setting controls all sounds, including notifications, alarms, and Siri responses. The volume level can also be adjusted directly from the **Control Center**:

    -   Swipe up on your watch face to open the **Control Center**.

    -   Tap the **volume icon** and adjust the slider to your preferred sound level.

2. **Using the Mute Function**
    If you prefer a more silent experience, you can mute your Apple Watch. This is useful in quiet environments, such as meetings, religious services, or when you're trying to avoid distractions.

    -   To mute your watch, open the **Control Center** and tap the **bell icon**. This will silence the sounds, although haptic alerts will still be active unless you choose to disable them.

    -   You can also mute the sound for specific apps, such as incoming messages, by adjusting the **Notifications settings**.

3. **Setting Up Alerts and Notifications**
    You can customize the types of notifications you receive on your Apple Watch. Whether it's for messages, emails, or calendar events, you can choose to receive alerts via sound, vibration, or both. This flexibility ensures that you're always aware of important updates without feeling overwhelmed by unnecessary notifications.

Adjusting Haptics: Tactile Feedback for Easier Use

Haptic feedback refers to the vibrations or tactile responses you feel on your wrist when interacting with the watch. This feature is especially helpful for seniors who may have difficulty hearing or seeing alerts. By adjusting the strength of the haptic feedback, you can ensure that you are always aware of incoming notifications.

1. **Changing Haptic Strength**

   To adjust the haptic feedback on your Apple Watch, go to **Settings > Sounds & Haptics**. You'll see an option to adjust the **haptic strength**. You can set it to a level that feels most comfortable for you, whether you prefer a gentle tap or a more intense vibration.

2. **Prominent Haptics**

   If you often miss notifications, you can enable **Prominent Haptics** to make the vibration more noticeable. This feature increases the strength and duration of the haptic feedback, ensuring you feel every alert clearly.

   - To turn on **Prominent Haptics**, go to **Settings > Sounds & Haptics**, and toggle the **Prominent Haptics** option to **On**.

3. **Haptic Feedback for Notifications**

   The Apple Watch automatically provides haptic feedback for incoming notifications, including calls, messages, and reminders. You can also set the watch to vibrate only for certain notifications, such as messages from loved ones or reminders about medication.

Adjusting Screen Brightness and Display Settings

For seniors with vision concerns, adjusting the **screen brightness** and **display settings** on the Apple Watch can make a significant difference. Whether you have trouble seeing small text or prefer a more vibrant display, Apple Watch allows you to make the screen as visible and clear as possible.

1. **Adjusting Brightness**

   To increase or decrease the screen brightness on your Apple Watch, go to **Settings > Brightness & Text Size**. Here, you'll see a slider that lets you control the brightness of the display. You can adjust it to your preference, ensuring that the screen is easy to read in different lighting conditions.

2. **Enabling Night Mode**

   If you're using your Apple Watch in low-light environments, such as in bed, you can activate **Nightstand Mode**. This dimly lit mode reduces screen brightness and turns your Apple Watch into a bedside clock.

○ Simply place your watch on its charger, and the watch will automatically switch to Nightstand Mode when the screen is idle.

3. **Text Size and Bold Text**

If you have trouble reading small text, you can increase the **text size** on your Apple Watch. To adjust this, go to **Settings > Display & Brightness** and tap **Text Size**. You can increase the size of the text for notifications, apps, and messages, making everything easier to read.

○ Additionally, you can enable **Bold Text** for a more prominent display, improving legibility.

Accessibility Settings: Larger Text, VoiceOver & More

Apple understands the importance of accessibility for seniors and has built a range of settings into the Apple Watch that can help you adapt the device to match your individual needs. From larger font to VoiceOver (a screen reader), Apple offers a comprehensive suite of accessibility features that make the Apple Watch more usable for persons with visual, hearing, and mobility issues.

Larger Text

For seniors who may have trouble reading small text, the Apple Watch offers a feature to **increase text size**, making it easier to read notifications, messages, and other app content.

1. **Increasing Text Size**

To change the text size, go to **Settings > Display & Brightness > Text Size**. Use the slider to adjust the text to a comfortable size. Larger text makes reading easier and helps reduce eye strain.

2. **Enabling Bold Text**

If you prefer a clearer, more visible text display, you can enable **Bold Text**. This will make the text more prominent and easier to read, especially for seniors with visual impairments. To enable this, go to **Settings > Accessibility** and toggle **Bold Text** on.

3. **Reducing Motion**

For seniors who may feel overwhelmed by fast-moving graphics or transitions on the screen, the **Reduce Motion** feature can simplify the watch's visual effects. To turn it on, go to **Settings > Accessibility > Reduce Motion** and toggle the option on.

VoiceOver: The Screen Reader for the Visually Impaired

For seniors with **vision impairment**, **VoiceOver** is an essential tool. This feature allows you to interact with the Apple Watch using voice commands. When VoiceOver is enabled, the watch will read out loud the text on the screen, including notifications, menu options, and messages.

How to Enable and Use VoiceOver:

1. **Enable VoiceOver**
   To enable VoiceOver on your Apple Watch, go to **Settings > Accessibility > VoiceOver** and toggle it on. Once VoiceOver is activated, the Apple Watch will read aloud the text and content on the screen as you interact with it.

2. **VoiceOver Gestures**
   After enabling VoiceOver, you can use gestures to navigate through the watch. To scroll, swipe up or down with two fingers. To select an item, tap twice with one finger. For seniors, learning these gestures can make interacting with the watch more intuitive.

3. **Speech Settings**
   In the **Accessibility** settings, you can also adjust the **speech rate** (the speed at which VoiceOver reads the text) and **voice settings** (to choose different voices or accents). This customization ensures that the reading pace is comfortable for your listening preference.

Zoom: Magnifying the Screen

If you have low vision but don't want to enable VoiceOver, the **Zoom** feature on Apple Watch allows you to magnify the screen for a closer look. This is especially helpful when reading text or looking at images that are hard to see.

How to Use Zoom:

1. **Enable Zoom**
   To enable **Zoom**, go to **Settings > Accessibility > Zoom** and toggle it on. Once activated, you can double-tap with two fingers to zoom in on any part of the screen.

2. **Zoom Options**
   You can adjust the zoom level to suit your needs. To zoom in, double-tap the screen with two fingers, and to zoom out, double-tap again. You can move around the screen by dragging with two fingers.

Sound and Visual Alerts for Hearing Impairments

The Apple Watch also offers features for seniors with hearing impairments. These settings include the ability to set visual alerts for incoming notifications and calls, as well as **haptic feedback** for alerts.

Enabling Visual and Haptic Alerts:

1. **Enable Haptic Alerts**
   If you have trouble hearing notifications, you can rely on **haptic feedback** (vibration). To enable haptic alerts, go to **Settings > Sounds & Haptics** and toggle on the **Haptic Alerts** option.

2. **Visual Alerts**
   For those with significant hearing impairments, enabling **visual notifications** can make a big difference. You can customize how alerts are displayed on your Apple Watch—whether they're large banners or colored indicators.

Creating Shortcuts for Daily Use

The Shortcuts app on your iPhone and Apple Watch allows you to create personalized automations and quick actions for frequently used tasks. This feature saves you time by enabling you to accomplish complex activities with a single tap or voice command.

What Are Shortcuts?

Shortcuts are actions that enable you to operate your Apple Watch and iPhone with a single command. Whether it's sending a text, accessing an app, or controlling your smart home devices, shortcuts make daily chores easier and faster. You can create custom shortcuts based on your needs, such as initiating Do Not Disturb mode, sending a brief message, or checking the weather.

How to Create Shortcuts on Your Apple Watch:

1. **Open the Shortcuts App on Your iPhone**
   To begin creating a shortcut, open the **Shortcuts app** on your iPhone. If you don't have the app, you can download it from the **App Store**.

2. **Create a New Shortcut**
   Tap the + button in the app to create a new shortcut. You can choose from a list of actions, such as:

- **Sending a Message**: Create a shortcut to send a pre-written message to someone.

- **Opening an App**: You can set up a shortcut to open a frequently used app.

- **Controlling Music**: Set up a shortcut to start or stop music, adjust the volume, or skip tracks.

3. **Add the Shortcut to Your Watch**

   After creating the shortcut on your iPhone, you can add it to your Apple Watch. Go to **Shortcuts > All Shortcuts** on your iPhone, and tap on the **Apple Watch icon** to sync it. This allows you to access the shortcut directly from your watch.

4. **Activate Shortcuts with Siri**

   You can also use **Siri** to activate your shortcuts. Simply say, "Hey Siri, [shortcut name]", and Siri will run the shortcut for you.

Personalizing your Apple Watch Series 10 is a vital step toward making it operate for you in the most comfortable and effective way possible. From altering audio, haptics, and brightness to tweaking accessibility settings and creating shortcuts for daily tasks, Apple Watch offers a variety of choices that allow you to adapt the device to your preferences.

Whether you're modifying text sizes for better reading, setting up visual alerts for greater hearing accessibility, or creating shortcuts for quick access to your favorite functions, these capabilities help make the Apple Watch Series 10 a strong tool that suits your needs.

By personalizing your Apple Watch, you boost not simply the functionality of the gadget, but also your overall experience with it. In the following chapter, we will explore the advanced health and fitness features of the Apple Watch Series 10, including heart rate monitoring, ECG, and sleep tracking, to ensure you're making the most out of your watch's health benefits.

Chapter 8

Exploring Essential Apps

The Apple Watch Series 10 is more than simply a fitness tracker or a notification gadget. It's a strong and adaptable companion meant to help you stay connected, informed, and entertained throughout the day. One of the primary aspects that make the Apple Watch genuinely stand out is its ability to effortlessly interact with critical apps that make daily living more comfortable and pleasurable. Whether it's checking the weather, receiving directions, listening to your favorite music, or making secure payments, the Apple Watch offers a range of apps that help you stay on top of life's tasks.

In this chapter, we'll explore some of the most useful apps accessible on your Apple Watch Series 10. We'll go into how to use the Weather app, get accurate and real-time updates with Maps and Compass, enjoy music and podcasts with ease, and make use of Apple Pay and other Wallet features to simplify your life.

By learning five crucial apps, you'll unlock the full potential of your Apple Watch, turning it into a powerful tool that goes beyond fitness and health tracking.

Using Weather, Maps, and Compass

Weather: Stay Informed About Your Surroundings

For seniors, keeping track of the weather is more than simply a convenience—it's vital for making informed decisions about everyday activities. Whether you're intending to go for a stroll, attend an outdoor event, or simply want to know how to dress for the day, the Weather app on the Apple Watch gives all the information you need, right at your fingertips.

How to Use the Weather App

1. **Opening the Weather App** To open the **Weather app** on your Apple Watch, press the **Digital Crown** to go to your Home Screen and tap the **Weather icon**. This will bring up a simple, easy-to-read interface showing the current temperature, weather conditions, and a brief forecast for the day.

2. **Viewing Hourly and Daily Forecasts** The **Weather app** provides a wealth of information that's accessible in just a few taps:

   o **Current Conditions**: The first thing you'll see is the current temperature, along with conditions such as sunny, cloudy, rainy, or snowy. You'll also get a quick overview of the **feels-like temperature**, which accounts for wind and humidity.

   o **Hourly Forecast**: If you want to know how the weather will change throughout the day, simply scroll down to see the hourly forecast. This gives you a look at the temperature, conditions, and expected weather for the next several hours.

   o **Daily Forecast**: The app also provides a summary of the upcoming days, showing high and low temperatures, as well as any expected weather events like rain or snow.

3. **Weather Alerts** You can enable **weather alerts** to stay informed about severe conditions like thunderstorms, high winds, or heavy rain. These alerts can be sent as notifications directly to your watch, helping you stay prepared. To set up alerts:

   o Open the **Weather app** on your iPhone and go to **Settings > Notifications**. You can customize which alerts you want to receive, such as **rain, snow, severe weather warnings**, and more.

4. **Using Complications to Access Weather Quickly** For quicker access to weather information, you can add a **weather complication** to your watch face. This lets you see the current temperature or a forecast directly on your watch face, without needing to open the app.

Weather App for Seniors

For seniors, the **Weather app** can be invaluable in helping you plan your day, especially if you have outdoor activities planned. It's important to stay informed about the weather, particularly during extreme conditions such as heatwaves, cold fronts, or storms. The Apple Watch's weather feature provides simple, easy-to-read data with large text, making it easier for seniors with visual impairments to stay informed.

Maps: Find Your Way with Ease

Whether you're heading out for a walk, a drive, or a trip to a new location, the **Maps app** on your Apple Watch helps you find your way with turn-by-turn directions. It provides both walking and driving navigation, so whether you're heading to a nearby park or navigating to a doctor's appointment, Maps keeps you on track.

How to Use the Maps App

1. **Opening the Maps App** The Maps app is available directly on your Apple Watch. To open it, press the **Digital Crown** to access the Home Screen, then tap the **Maps app** (the icon looks like a map). You can also use **Siri** to ask for directions, such as "Hey Siri, how do I get to the nearest grocery store?"

2. **Getting Directions** To get directions, you can either type in your destination or ask Siri for help. Here's how to do it:

   - **Using Siri**: Say, "Hey Siri, get directions to [destination]," and Siri will find the best route for you. Once the directions are loaded, the watch will provide turn-by-turn guidance, either via **haptic feedback** (vibrations on your wrist) or audio cues if you have your sound on.

   - **Manual Search**: You can also search for a place directly in the Maps app. Simply tap the search bar, enter the address or the place you want to visit, and the app will show you directions.

3. **Walking Directions** For seniors who prefer walking over driving, the **Maps app** also provides walking directions. These directions offer clear, step-by-step guidance, helping you get to your destination safely, whether it's a local park, a shopping center, or a neighbor's house.

4. **Viewing Traffic and Estimated Time of Arrival** The **Maps app** on your Apple Watch also provides real-time traffic information, helping you adjust your plans in case of delays. You'll see the **estimated time of arrival (ETA)** based on traffic conditions, which is incredibly helpful if you have time-sensitive appointments.

5. **Using Complications for Quick Access** You can add a **Maps complication** to your watch face for quick access to directions. With just a glance, you'll be able to see your next turn or your ETA, keeping you on track while you're on the go.

Maps for Seniors

For seniors, the **Maps app** can be a lifesaver, especially if you're traveling to new or unfamiliar locations. The **turn-by-turn navigation** and **haptic feedback** make it easier to follow directions without needing to look at your watch constantly. It's a great way to ensure you stay safe and on course, whether walking or driving.

Compass: Find Your Bearings

The **Compass app** on the Apple Watch Series 10 is a handy tool that helps you understand where you are and which direction you're heading. Whether you're out hiking, exploring a new city, or just curious about your surroundings, the Compass app gives you the tools to find your way.

How to Use the Compass App

1. **Opening the Compass App** Open the **Compass app** by pressing the **Digital Crown**, then tap on the **Compass icon** (which resembles a compass rose). Once open, you'll see a digital compass that shows the cardinal directions (North, South, East, and West), along with your current heading and location.

2. **Using the Compass for Hiking or Outdoor Activities** If you're out hiking or walking in unfamiliar terrain, the Compass app can help you stay oriented. The app will show you your **current bearing**, so you know exactly where you're headed. You can also use it to check if you're heading in the right direction toward a specific location.

3. **Adding Elevation Information** The Compass app on the Apple Watch Series 10 also includes your **altitude**, which is helpful for activities like hiking or climbing. This feature can tell you how high you are above sea level, giving you additional context about your surroundings.

4. **Using Compass with Maps** The Compass app can be used in conjunction with the **Maps app** to give you even more accurate navigation. By combining these tools, you can make sure you're on the right path, especially when hiking or venturing into the wilderness.

Compass for Seniors

For seniors who enjoy outdoor activities like hiking or walking, the **Compass app** offers peace of mind. It helps you maintain orientation in unfamiliar environments, making it easier to explore confidently.

Listening to Music, Podcasts, and Audiobooks

One of the most fun features of the Apple Watch Series 10 is its capacity to keep you occupied, whether you're at home, on a stroll, or traveling. With apps like Apple Music, Podcasts, and Audiobooks, you can listen to your favorite tracks, catch up on podcasts, or enjoy an audiobook—all from your wrist.

Using Apple Music on Your Apple Watch

Apple Music offers a large catalog of music, from old classics to the latest releases. With the Apple Watch, you can stream or download your favorite songs and playlists, making it a wonderful alternative for staying occupied while working out, relaxing, or doing errands.

1. **Listening to Music** To listen to music, open the **Music app** on your Apple Watch. You can sync playlists, albums, and songs from your **Apple Music** library directly to your watch. Once synced, you can listen to music even when your iPhone isn't nearby.

2. **Playing Music with AirPods** For a more immersive listening experience, connect your **AirPods** (or any Bluetooth headphones) to your Apple Watch. Once paired, you can control playback directly from the watch, adjusting volume, skipping tracks, and pausing the music.

3. **Creating Playlists** You can create playlists on your **iPhone** and sync them to your Apple Watch. This allows you to easily access your favorite tunes without needing to use your phone.

Listening to Podcasts on Your Apple Watch

Podcasts are a great way to stay informed, entertained, and inspired. With the **Podcasts app**, you can listen to your favorite shows directly from your Apple Watch. Whether it's news, storytelling, or comedy, podcasts offer endless content to explore.

1. **Listening to Podcasts** To listen to podcasts, open the **Podcasts app** on your Apple Watch and browse your subscribed shows. You can stream episodes or download them for offline listening.

2. **Managing Playback** The Podcasts app on the Apple Watch allows you to control playback—pause, play, skip, or rewind—directly from your wrist. It's the perfect solution for listening on the go, whether you're out for a walk or working out.

Listening to Audiobooks

For seniors who love reading but find it difficult to sit down with a book, **audiobooks** are a fantastic option. The Apple Watch Series 10 makes it easy to listen to audiobooks while still being mobile and active.

1. **Using the Books App** The **Books app** on your Apple Watch allows you to listen to audiobooks you've purchased or downloaded. To start, open the **Books app** and select an audiobook to begin listening.

2. **Syncing Audiobooks from iPhone** You can sync audiobooks from your **iPhone** to your Apple Watch by using the **Books app** on your iPhone. Once synced, you can listen directly from your Apple Watch using Bluetooth headphones or the watch's built-in speaker.

Using Wallet: Apple Pay, Tickets, and More

The **Wallet app** on your Apple Watch is an essential tool for managing payments, tickets, boarding passes, and more. With Apple Pay, you can make secure payments directly from your wrist, without needing to take out your wallet or phone.

Using Apple Pay on Your Apple Watch

Apple Pay allows you to make secure, contactless payments with just a tap of your Apple Watch. It's a fast and secure way to pay for groceries, coffee, or anything else that supports contactless payment.

1. **Setting Up Apple Pay** To set up **Apple Pay**, open the **Wallet app** on your iPhone and follow the steps to add your credit or debit card. Once added, the cards will sync with your Apple Watch, allowing you to make payments directly from your wrist.

2. **Making Payments with Apple Pay** To make a payment, double-tap the **Side Button** on your Apple Watch to bring up your default card. Hold your watch near the payment terminal, and it will automatically complete the transaction.

3. **Using Apple Pay for Transit** In some cities, you can also use **Apple Pay** for **transit fares**. Simply tap your watch on the transit reader, and the payment will be processed.

Storing Tickets and Boarding Passes

In addition to payments, the **Wallet app** also allows you to store important items like **tickets**, **boarding passes**, and **loyalty cards**.

1. **Adding Tickets and Boarding Passes** You can add tickets and passes to your Apple Watch by saving them to the **Wallet app** on your iPhone. When you're ready, simply open the **Wallet app** on your Apple Watch to view your tickets or boarding passes.

2. **Accessing Tickets Easily** Your Apple Watch will display your tickets or passes with a simple tap. You can swipe between items, making it easy to find what you need when you're at an event, traveling, or using public transit.

The Apple Watch Series 10 is a versatile device that works as a fitness tracker, communication tool, and source of entertainment. With key apps like Weather, Maps, Music, and Wallet, your Apple Watch becomes a trustworthy companion throughout the day. These apps give practical solutions for remaining informed, entertained, and organized, helping you make the most out of your smartwatch experience.

Using Camera Remote and Photos

One of the more fascinating features of the Apple Watch Series 10 is the ability to manage your iPhone's camera remotely. This is a terrific tool for seniors who enjoy taking photos but may find it tough to hold the phone at the appropriate angle or hit the shutter button.

How the Camera Remote App Works

The Camera Remote software converts your Apple Watch into a viewfinder and shutter button for your iPhone's camera. With this software, you can frame your images from your wrist, offering you a unique angle and the ease of remote shooting. It's especially beneficial for selfies or group photographs if you want to be in the picture but don't want to ask someone else to shoot the photo.

How to Use the Camera Remote App

1. **Open the Camera Remote App**
   To start, press the **Digital Crown** on your Apple Watch to open the **Home Screen**, and then tap the **Camera Remote app**. This will launch the camera app on your iPhone.

2. **Frame Your Shot**

Once the Camera Remote app is open on your Apple Watch, you'll see a **live view** of what your iPhone camera is seeing. You can adjust your position and angle from your wrist, ensuring that you frame your shot exactly as you want it.

3. **Take the Photo**

When you're ready to take the photo, tap the **Shutter button** on your Apple Watch. You'll see a 3-second countdown on the watch to give you time to get into position before the photo is taken.

4. **Use the Timer**

If you want to take a photo with a little more preparation time, you can enable the **timer** feature. The Apple Watch allows you to set a timer for 3 or 10 seconds, giving you time to get into the right pose before the camera snaps the picture.

5. **Zoom and Focus**

For added control, the Camera Remote app allows you to zoom in or out and adjust the focus directly from your Apple Watch. This is great for taking portraits, close-up shots, or when you want to ensure the camera focuses on a specific area.

Why the Camera Remote App Is Useful for Seniors

For seniors who appreciate photography, this app is a game-changer. It eliminates the necessity for physically handling the iPhone when shooting images. The remote control feature allows you to record moments easily, without struggling to click the shutter button. Whether you're taking photos at family gatherings, during travel, or just snapping a selfie, the Camera Remote app enables you to accomplish it effortlessly.

Using the Photos App on Your Apple Watch

In addition to operating your iPhone's camera, the Apple Watch Series 10 allows you to browse and manage your Photos directly from your wrist. Whether you want to look back on fond memories, browse through albums, or select a photo to use as your watch face, the Photos app makes it easy to enjoy your photos on the go.

How to View Photos on Your Apple Watch

1. **Syncing Photos with Your Watch**

To sync photos with your Apple Watch, open the **Apple Watch app** on your iPhone, go to **My Watch**, then tap **Photos**. You can choose which albums you want to sync with your watch, or you can select a specific number of photos to be stored on your device.

2. **Viewing Photos on the Watch**
   Once the photos are synced, open the **Photos app** on your Apple Watch. You'll see a selection of the images you synced from your iPhone. You can scroll through them by swiping left or right, and tap any image to view it in full-screen mode.

3. **Setting a Photo as Your Watch Face**
   One of the most personal ways to use the Photos app is by setting a photo as your **watch face**. To do this, open the **Photos app** on your Apple Watch, select your favorite photo, and choose **Set as Watch Face**. This allows you to carry your memories with you every time you check the time.

Why Photos Matter for Seniors

For seniors, having ready access to beloved memories can bring delight and comfort throughout the day. Whether it's images of loved ones, pets, or memorable occasions, displaying your favorite photos as your watch face helps you to keep these memories close. Additionally, the option to view images on your wrist offers a convenient method to reminisce without having to go through your phone or computer.

News, Stocks, and Other Information Apps

Your Apple Watch Series 10 isn't just about fitness and communication—it also helps you keep informed with real-time updates on news, stocks, and other essential information. These apps allow you to rapidly check the latest headlines, watch stock prices, and keep in the loop on the go.

Using the News App

The News app on the Apple Watch offers the latest headlines and updates right to your wrist. With this software, you may get breaking news, follow specific areas of interest, and keep informed without needing to open your iPhone or go through social media.

How to Use the News App

1. **Opening the News App**
   To open the **News app** on your Apple Watch, press the **Digital Crown** to go to the Home Screen, and tap the **News app icon**. You'll see a list of the latest headlines and top stories from your preferred news sources.

2. **Browsing News Stories**

   Once you open the app, you can scroll through the latest stories by swiping up or down. Tap on a headline to read the full article. The app gives you a preview of the story and lets you decide if you want to dive deeper or just get a quick update.

3. **Setting Up Notifications**

   You can also receive **notifications** for breaking news or stories related to your interests. To customize notifications, open the **News app** on your iPhone, go to **Settings > Notifications**, and choose which types of stories you'd like to be alerted about.

Why the News App is Important for Seniors

Staying informed is vital, and the News app on the Apple Watch makes it easy to scan headlines and get updates without getting overwhelmed. For seniors, it's a way to keep connected with the world around them, especially when on the go or during leisure. The tiny design guarantees you can view the latest headlines quickly, and notifications keep you updated on key occurrences.

Using the Stocks App

The **Stocks app** on the Apple Watch helps you track the performance of your stocks, bonds, and other investments in real-time. For seniors who manage their finances or like to keep an eye on the markets, this app provides valuable information at a glance.

How to Use the Stocks App

1. **Opening the Stocks App**

   To open the **Stocks app**, press the **Digital Crown** on your Apple Watch and tap the **Stocks app icon**. The app will show you the current market performance of the stocks you've added.

2. **Adding Stocks to Your Watch**

   To add stocks, open the **Stocks app** on your iPhone and choose the stocks you want to follow. They will sync with your Apple Watch, and you can check them at any time.

3. **Viewing Stock Data**

   The Stocks app shows you the **current price**, **change in value**, **percentage change**, and **historical data** for each stock. You can also tap on a stock to see a detailed chart with real-time data.

4. **Setting Up Alerts**

   For seniors who like to stay on top of stock market fluctuations, you can set **price alerts** for specific stocks. To do this, open the **Stocks app** on your iPhone and set the alert for a price threshold. When the stock hits that threshold, you'll receive a notification on your Apple Watch.

Why the Stocks App is Useful for Seniors

The Stocks app offers seniors a simple way to stay updated on their investments and financial markets. Whether you're actively managing your portfolio or just want to check in on your stocks, this app allows you to track your financial performance easily and at your convenience.

Using Other Information Apps

Apple Watch also provides several other **information apps** that help you manage daily tasks, stay organized, and track important events. These include apps for your calendar, reminders, weather, and more.

- **Calendar**: The Calendar app keeps you on track with important appointments and events. You can quickly check upcoming meetings, doctor's appointments, and social gatherings. The app syncs with your iPhone's calendar, ensuring you never miss an important date.

- **Reminders**: This app helps you keep track of your to-do list and set reminders for essential tasks. Whether it's picking up groceries or taking medication, the Reminders app ensures you stay on top of your daily responsibilities.

- **Weather**: The Weather app on the Apple Watch gives you quick access to weather updates. Whether you're planning a walk or getting ready for the day, knowing the forecast ensures you're prepared for changing conditions.

Finding and Downloading Apps from the App Store

The **App Store** on the Apple Watch offers a wide range of apps designed to enhance your Apple Watch experience. Whether you're looking for fitness apps, entertainment apps, or productivity tools, the App Store has something for everyone.

How to Find and Download Apps

1. **Opening the App Store**
   Press the **Digital Crown** on your Apple Watch and tap the **App Store icon** to browse available apps.

2. **Searching for Apps**
   You can search for apps by typing in the name of the app or browsing through categories such as **Fitness, Health, Entertainment, Travel**, and more.

3. **Downloading Apps**
   Once you find an app you like, tap on it, then select **Get** or **Install** to download it directly to your Apple Watch. Some apps are free, while others may require a purchase or subscription.

4. **Installing Apps on Your iPhone First**
   Many apps are designed to work on both your iPhone and Apple Watch. To install these apps on your iPhone first, download them from the **iPhone App Store**, and they will automatically sync to your Apple Watch.

Why Download Apps for Apple Watch?

Downloading apps from the **App Store** adds more functionality to your Apple Watch. Whether it's a specialized app for managing your health, learning new skills, or staying connected with loved ones, these apps enhance the capabilities of your Apple Watch and help you live a more connected and organized life.

The Apple Watch Series 10 is packed with key apps that help you stay informed, engaged, and connected. From utilizing the Camera Remote and Photos applications to reading news, watching stocks, and finding new apps in the App Store, your Apple Watch becomes an invaluable tool for managing your everyday activities and interests.

By understanding five crucial apps, you can make your Apple Watch work even harder for you. Whether it's staying updated on the latest headlines, capturing memories with family, or staying on top of your finances, the Apple Watch Series 10 is more than just a watch—it's a complete lifestyle assistant.

Chapter 9

Staying Safe and Secure

In a world where our devices collect and manage personal information, privacy and security have never been more crucial. With the Apple Watch Series 10, you have a powerful tool that keeps you connected to the world around you, but it's also necessary to guarantee that your data and personal information are protected. Whether you're using your watch for communication, tracking your fitness, or making payments, you need peace of mind that your device is secure.

Apple has fitted the Apple Watch Series 10 with a variety of technologies aimed to keep your watch and data safe. From setting up passcodes to using Find My Watch in case of loss or theft, and configuring privacy settings, you can take charge of your security and guarantee that your watch runs in a safe and secure manner. This chapter will guide you through the important features and settings that will help you protect your Apple Watch.

Setting Up Passwords and Security Settings

The Apple Watch Series 10 is designed with security in mind, and one of the first steps in safeguarding your device is setting up a passcode. This simple but effective security solution adds an extra layer of protection to your watch, guaranteeing that only you can access its capabilities and data. Whether you're using the watch for personal chores, communication, or health tracking, a passcode is the first step toward securing your privacy.

Why a Passcode is Important

Setting a passcode on your Apple Watch ensures that no one may access your information if your watch is lost or stolen. The passcode feature locks your device, so even if someone else attempts to use it, they will be unable to access your personal apps, messages, or health data. Additionally, a passcode is required to utilize specific functions, such as Apple Pay and the Wallet app, to prevent illegal transactions.

For elderly, having a passcode is very vital. It ensures that any sensitive information kept on the watch—such as medical data, personal contacts, and payment details—remains private and secure.

How to Set Up a Passcode

Setting up a passcode on your Apple Watch is a straightforward process. Here's how you can do it:

1. **Open the Settings App**
   Press the **Digital Crown** to access your **Home Screen**, then tap the **Settings** icon (gear-shaped).

2. **Select Passcode**
   Scroll down and select **Passcode**. Tap on **Turn Passcode On**.

3. **Create a Passcode**
   You'll be prompted to create a passcode. Choose a passcode that is easy for you to remember but difficult for others to guess. For enhanced security, it's best to use a **6-digit passcode**, but you can also choose a 4-digit passcode if you prefer.

4. **Re-enter the Passcode**
   After entering your passcode, you'll need to **re-enter it** to confirm.

5. **Enable or Disable Features**
   Once the passcode is set, you can also enable or disable additional features related to your watch's security. For example, you can activate **Erase Data** to automatically erase all data on the watch after 10 failed passcode attempts. This adds an extra layer of security if your watch is lost or stolen.

Customizing Security Settings

In addition to setting up a passcode, Apple Watch provides other options for securing your device:

1. **Wrist Detection**
   The Apple Watch has a feature called **Wrist Detection**, which ensures that the watch remains locked unless it is being worn. When you remove the watch from your wrist, it will automatically lock, preventing unauthorized access to the watch's features. To turn this feature on, go to **Settings > Passcode**, then toggle on **Wrist Detection**.

2. **Unlocking with iPhone**
   If you prefer not to enter your passcode every time you put your Apple Watch on, you can set your iPhone to automatically unlock the watch. This feature requires that your **iPhone** be unlocked with Face ID or Touch ID, and your **Apple Watch** will automatically unlock as well. To enable this, go to **Settings > Passcode > Unlock with iPhone**.

3. **Locking Your Watch Manually**

   If you want to manually lock your Apple Watch, you can do so from the **Control Center**. Swipe up from the bottom of your watch's face to open the **Control Center**, then tap the **lock icon**. This will lock your watch until you enter your passcode.

Using Find My Watch

Losing your Apple Watch can be distressing, especially if it contains vital information like medical data, contacts, or financial information. Fortunately, Apple includes a service called Find My that can help you locate your watch if it's lost or misplaced. The Find My Watch feature works in conjunction with Find My iPhone and can be accessed from either your Apple Watch or iPhone.

How to Set Up Find My Watch

1. **Enable Find My on Your iPhone**
   The first step is to ensure that **Find My iPhone** is enabled on your iPhone, as this will also activate **Find My Watch**. To enable **Find My iPhone**, go to **Settings > [your name] > iCloud**, then toggle on **Find My iPhone** and **Send Last Location**.

2. **Activate Find My Watch**
   Once Find My iPhone is enabled, your Apple Watch will automatically be connected to the **Find My** app. To confirm that Find My Watch is set up, go to the **Find My app** on your iPhone, and you'll see your Apple Watch listed under your devices.

3. **Locate Your Watch**
   If you lose your watch, open the **Find My app** on your iPhone or visit the **iCloud website** on any computer. Select your Apple Watch from the list of devices, and you'll see its **last known location** on a map. If your watch is nearby, you can play a sound to help locate it.

4. **Mark as Lost**
   If you can't find your watch right away, you can activate **Lost Mode**. This will lock the device and display a custom message with your contact information on the screen. You can also choose to receive a notification when the watch is found.

5. **Erasing Your Watch Remotely**
   If you believe your watch has been stolen or can't be recovered, you can erase all data remotely to protect your privacy. In the **Find My** app, select your Apple Watch and

choose **Erase This Device**. This will wipe all information from your watch, ensuring that your personal data remains secure.

Privacy Settings for Seniors

As a senior, maintaining your privacy is especially important, and Apple has designed several settings on the Apple Watch to help you keep your personal information safe. Apple offers robust privacy settings that allow you to control what data is shared and with whom.

Managing Notifications and Privacy

Your Apple Watch alerts you to incoming notifications, including messages, calls, and app updates. However, you may not always want others to see this information, especially in public spaces. Apple Watch gives you several options to ensure your notifications remain private.

1. **Hide Sensitive Information in Notifications**
   You can adjust your notification settings to ensure that sensitive information (like email content or text messages) is hidden when you receive notifications. Go to **Settings > Notifications**, then choose the app for which you want to adjust settings. Toggle on **Show Previews** and set it to **Never** or **When Unlocked**.

2. **Do Not Disturb Mode**
   If you don't want to be disturbed by notifications at a specific time, you can use **Do Not Disturb** mode. This feature silences all incoming notifications, calls, and alerts. To enable it, swipe up on your watch face to open the **Control Center**, then tap the **crescent moon icon**. You can also schedule Do Not Disturb mode for specific times, such as during sleep or meetings.

3. **Locking Notifications Screen**
   To prevent others from seeing your notifications when your watch is unlocked, you can lock your screen after receiving notifications. Go to **Settings > Notifications**, and choose **Notification Privacy**. This will ensure that notifications remain private, even when you check them quickly.

Managing Health Data Privacy

Your Apple Watch collects sensitive health data, including heart rate, exercise routines, sleep patterns, and more. Apple takes your privacy seriously and allows you to control how this data is shared and stored.

1. **Health App Privacy**

    The **Health app** on your iPhone allows you to track all your health and fitness data. Apple uses **end-to-end encryption** to protect this data, so only you have access to it. You can control which apps have access to your health data by going to **Settings > Health > Data Access & Devices**. From here, you can grant or revoke permissions for individual apps.

2. **Sharing Health Data with Doctors**

    If you wish to share your health data with your healthcare provider, you can use the **Health app** to create a secure sharing link. Go to **Health > Sharing** and select **Share with Doctor** to send a summary of your health metrics.

3. **Emergency Medical ID**

    The **Medical ID** feature on your Apple Watch allows first responders to access critical health information in case of an emergency. To set this up, open the **Health app** on your iPhone, tap **Medical ID**, and enter relevant medical details like allergies, conditions, and medications. You can also choose to share this information with emergency services.

Keeping your Apple Watch Series 10 secure and private is vital for protecting your personal information. By setting up a passcode, using Find My Watch, and configuring privacy settings, you can ensure that your device remains secure and that your sensitive data is secured. Whether you're monitoring notifications, regulating access to your health data, or using the Find My app to locate your watch, these options provide peace of mind and control over your device.

Family Setup: Managing Watches for Loved Ones

What is Family Setup?

Family Setup is a significant function supplied by Apple, allowing you to manage and set up Apple Watches for family members who may not have an iPhone. This includes youngsters, elderly parents, or other folks who benefit from having an Apple Watch but don't require or want the full capability of an iPhone. With Family Setup, you can provide loved ones the independence and connectivity of an Apple Watch while maintaining control over key settings.

For elders, Family Setup can be particularly advantageous if you wish to maintain access to safety features, health monitoring, and communication, without needing to possess a smartphone. It allows a caregiver or family member to set up an Apple Watch for a loved one and manage it remotely.

Setting Up Family Setup

If you have an Apple Watch Series 10 and want to manage another watch through Family Setup, here's how you can do it:

1. Requirements for Family Setup

Before setting up Family Setup, you need the following:

- **An iPhone** running **iOS 14 or later**.

- **An Apple Watch Series 4 or later** with **watchOS 7 or later**.

- **A Family member's Apple Watch** (can be for a child or senior) that does not yet have an iPhone.

2. How to Set Up Family Setup on Your iPhone

1. **Open the Apple Watch App**
   On your iPhone, open the **Apple Watch app**. This is the app used to pair and manage Apple Watches. Tap on **All Watches** at the top of the screen.

2. **Add a Family Member's Watch**
   Tap on **Add Watch,** then select **Set Up for a Family Member**. The app will guide you through the setup process.

3. **Pair the Watch**
   Hold the Apple Watch near your iPhone and follow the on-screen instructions to pair the watch. This involves positioning the Apple Watch's screen inside the viewfinder of your iPhone's camera.

4. **Set Up the Watch**
   During setup, you'll be prompted to choose whether the person wearing the watch is a **child** or a **senior**. Based on this selection, you'll have access to specific settings for safety, privacy, and health.

5. **Customize Settings for the Family Member**
   Once paired, you can customize settings such as:

   - **Location sharing**: You can track the location of the Apple Watch, ensuring that you always know where your loved one is.

- **Schooltime**: For children, you can set up **Schooltime** mode, which restricts app usage and notifications during school hours.

- **Health monitoring**: For seniors, you can enable important health features, like heart rate tracking and emergency alerts.

6. **Configure Communication**

   You can manage the watch's ability to make and receive calls, send messages, and receive notifications. With Family Setup, your loved one can communicate with you directly from their watch, even if they don't have an iPhone.

7. **Setting Up Apple Cash**

   If the Apple Watch is for a child, you can set up **Apple Cash** to allow them to make payments, receive allowances, or use the watch for small purchases. The Family Organizer (you) controls the funding and limits on Apple Cash.

What You Can Manage with Family Setup

Once the watch is set up for your family member, you can manage and monitor the following aspects remotely:

- **Health Data**: For seniors, the watch can track vital signs such as heart rate, and you can receive notifications if something abnormal is detected.

- **Activity Monitoring**: You can monitor steps, exercise, and sleep data, ensuring your loved ones stay active and healthy.

- **Communication**: As the Family Organizer, you can control which contacts your family member can communicate with on the Apple Watch.

Why Family Setup is Valuable for Seniors

Family Setup provides seniors with the independence and freedom of owning an Apple Watch, without the need for an iPhone. For seniors, this means:

- **Easier Communication**: You can stay in touch with family members without needing to handle complicated smartphones.

- **Safety**: With features like **Emergency SOS**, **Fall Detection**, and the ability to share locations, Family Setup offers peace of mind for caregivers.

- **Health Monitoring**: Seniors can benefit from automatic health tracking, including heart rate monitoring and emergency alerts, making it easier for family members to keep track of their well-being.

Family Setup is a great tool for caregivers and family members who want to ensure their loved ones stay safe, connected, and healthy, all while allowing seniors the independence to use the Apple Watch on their own.

Understanding and Using Emergency SOS Features

In emergency situations, having rapid access to support can make all the difference. The Emergency SOS feature on the Apple Watch Series 10 allows you to swiftly contact emergency services with just a push of a button, whether you are at home, on the go, or in an urgent circumstance.

What is Emergency SOS?

Emergency SOS is a safety feature that allows you to instantly call emergency services by pressing and holding the Side Button on your Apple Watch. When enabled, your Apple Watch will automatically contact emergency responders (e.g., 911) and send a message to your emergency contacts. It's designed to be utilized in instances where you may not have time to make a call manually or when you need help fast.

This feature is especially crucial for elderly who may be at a higher risk for falls or medical issues. With Emergency SOS, you may feel confident knowing that help is just a press away.

How to Use Emergency SOS

1. **Activate Emergency SOS**
   To activate **Emergency SOS** on your Apple Watch, press and hold the **Side Button** and the **Digital Crown** at the same time for about 5 seconds. You'll see a **slider** appear on the screen with an option to **slide to call emergency services**.

2. **Calling Emergency Services**
   If you're able to, slide the **Emergency SOS slider** to call for help. If you're unable to swipe, the watch will automatically place the call to emergency services after a few seconds.

3. **Send Your Location**
   Once you've called emergency services, your Apple Watch will send your current

location to the authorities. This is especially helpful if you're unable to speak or describe where you are, as emergency responders can locate you even if you can't give them your address.

4. **Alerting Emergency Contacts**
   After the emergency call is made, your Apple Watch will send a notification to your **emergency contacts** with your location and a message that you've activated Emergency SOS. This provides peace of mind for your family and loved ones, as they will be alerted immediately when you need help.

5. **Automatic Fall Detection**
   If your Apple Watch detects that you've had a fall and you don't respond to the prompt asking if you're okay, it will automatically initiate Emergency SOS. This is particularly useful for seniors who may fall and be unable to reach their phone.

Emergency SOS for Seniors

The **Emergency SOS** feature is an invaluable tool for seniors who want to stay safe. Whether it's a fall, medical emergency, or another urgent situation, being able to access help quickly can be a lifesaver. Seniors can activate the SOS feature even if they can't speak or don't have their phone nearby, as the Apple Watch provides all the necessary tools for getting help.

Customizing Emergency SOS Settings

You can customize certain aspects of the **Emergency SOS** feature to make sure it works exactly as you need it. Here's how you can manage the settings:

1. **Set Up Emergency Contacts**
   To make sure your family or friends are notified in case of an emergency, add emergency contacts in the **Health app** on your iPhone. These contacts will automatically be notified when Emergency SOS is activated.

   ○ Open the **Health app** on your iPhone.

   ○ Tap on **Medical ID**.

   ○ Select **Edit** and scroll down to **Emergency Contacts**.

   ○ Tap **Add Emergency Contact** and choose a contact from your address book.

2. **Activate Fall Detection**
   To enable **Fall Detection**, which automatically triggers Emergency SOS if a hard fall is

detected, go to **Settings > Emergency SOS** on your Apple Watch. Turn on **Fall Detection** by selecting **On**. This feature is particularly helpful for seniors who may be at a higher risk of falls.

3. **Using the Apple Watch's Silent Mode**

   If you don't want your Apple Watch to make a sound when Emergency SOS is activated, you can use **Silent Mode**. This can be enabled through the **Control Center**, which will keep your watch's display on but mute the sounds of incoming calls and notifications.

4. **Medical ID Setup**

   Ensure your **Medical ID** is set up on your iPhone so that emergency responders can access vital health information in case of an emergency. This includes allergies, medications, medical conditions, and blood type. Your **Medical ID** will be accessible even when your Apple Watch is locked.

The Apple Watch Series 10 includes powerful safety features that provide both seniors and their loved ones peace of mind. By setting up Family Setup, you can effortlessly manage Apple Watches for loved ones, ensuring they stay connected and safe. And in the event of an emergency, Emergency SOS is always ready to aid, whether it's from a fall, a medical issue, or any other critical scenario.

By employing these capabilities, seniors may enjoy the independence and benefits of the Apple Watch Series 10, knowing that they are always just a push of a button away from getting help when required. Family Setup also guarantees that caregivers and family members have the resources to help and monitor their loved ones, ensuring security and connection at all times.

Chapter 10

Troubleshooting and Common Fixes

The Apple Watch Series 10 is a sophisticated and feature-rich device, designed to make daily living easier, more organized, more connected. However, as with any piece of technology, there may be occasions when things don't perform as expected. Whether your watch is stalling, failing to connect to Wi-Fi, or not synchronizing with your iPhone, these issues can be aggravating.

Fortunately, the Apple Watch Series 10 is packed with many tools and options to help overcome common concerns. In this chapter, we'll guide you through a number of troubleshooting techniques and fixes to ensure your Apple Watch continues to perform at its best. We'll cover restarting and resetting your Apple Watch, resolving connectivity difficulties such as Wi-Fi, Bluetooth, and iPhone syncing problems, and troubleshooting typical notification issues.

By the end of this chapter, you'll be equipped with the knowledge and confidence to perform simple troubleshooting chores on your own, so you can continue to enjoy the full benefits of your Apple Watch.

Restarting and Resetting Your Apple Watch

Why Restarting Can Fix Common Issues

Restarting your Apple Watch can cure a wide range of problems, from slow performance to trouble with apps or connectivity. When you restart your device, it effectively gives it a fresh start by eliminating transient faults and freeing up memory. It's a simple and effective repair that can tackle many common difficulties without the need for more harsh procedures.

How to Restart Your Apple Watch

1. **Press and Hold the Side Button**
   To restart your Apple Watch, press and hold the **Side Button** (the long button on the right side of your watch) until the **Power Off slider** appears on the screen.

2. **Swipe to Power Off**
   Once the slider appears, swipe the slider from left to right to turn off your watch. This

process may take about 10 seconds, and your watch will power down completely.

3. **Turn the Watch Back On**
   After the watch has turned off, press and hold the **Side Button** again until the Apple logo appears on the screen. Your Apple Watch will restart, and once it powers back up, check to see if the issue you were experiencing is resolved.

When to Restart Your Watch

You should consider restarting your Apple Watch if:

- The watch feels slow or unresponsive.

- Apps are not opening or functioning properly.

- Your watch is not connected to Wi-Fi or Bluetooth.

- You experience a delay in receiving notifications.

- The screen is frozen or stuck on a particular screen.

Restarting the device often solves these problems and can save you time compared to more complex troubleshooting steps.

Resetting Your Apple Watch

In some cases, restarting may not be enough to fix the issue. If you are still experiencing problems, you may need to perform a **factory reset** on your Apple Watch. A factory reset erases all data from the device and restores it to its original settings, so it's important to back up your data before proceeding with this step.

How to Factory Reset Your Apple Watch

1. **Backup Your Data**
   Before resetting your Apple Watch, make sure that your data is backed up. Apple Watch data is automatically backed up to **iCloud** when it's paired with your iPhone, so once your iPhone is synced with your Apple Watch, your data is safe.

2. **Open the Settings App**
   On your Apple Watch, press the **Digital Crown** to open the Home Screen, then tap the **Settings** app (gear icon).

3. **Go to General**

   In the Settings menu, scroll down and tap on **General**.

4. **Reset**

   Scroll to the bottom and select **Reset**. Here, you'll have several options:

   - **Erase All Content and Settings**: This option will completely erase your Apple Watch and reset it to its factory settings. You'll be prompted to enter your passcode and confirm that you want to erase all data.

   - **Unpair Apple Watch**: If you prefer to reset your watch via your iPhone, open the **Apple Watch app** on your iPhone, go to the **My Watch** tab, and select **Unpair Apple Watch**. This will also erase all data and settings on your watch and unpair it from your iPhone.

5. **Confirm Reset**

   Once you confirm the reset, your watch will begin erasing all content. The process may take a few minutes. After the reset is complete, your Apple Watch will restart as if it were brand new, and you can set it up again from scratch.

When to Perform a Factory Reset

Consider resetting your Apple Watch if:

- The watch continues to experience issues after restarting, such as frozen apps or connection problems.

- You want to give the watch to someone else, and you need to erase all personal data.

- You are encountering persistent software issues that cannot be resolved by simpler troubleshooting methods.

Fixing Connectivity Issues (Wi-Fi, Bluetooth, iPhone Sync)

Connectivity issues can often be a major source of frustration. Whether your Apple Watch isn't connected to Wi-Fi, Bluetooth, or syncing with your iPhone, there are several steps you can take to resolve these problems.

Fixing Wi-Fi Connectivity Issues

If your Apple Watch is having trouble connecting to Wi-Fi, it can prevent you from accessing internet services and apps that require a connection. Here are some tips to fix Wi-Fi connectivity issues:

1. **Check Wi-Fi Settings**

    ○ On your iPhone, make sure that **Wi-Fi** is turned on and connected to a network. Your Apple Watch relies on your iPhone's connection to access Wi-Fi, so ensure that your iPhone is connected to a stable Wi-Fi network.

    ○ On your Apple Watch, swipe up on the watch face to open the **Control Center**, and ensure that the **Wi-Fi** icon is highlighted. This indicates that your watch is connected to Wi-Fi.

2. **Reconnect to Wi-Fi**
    If your Apple Watch isn't connecting to Wi-Fi, you can try disconnecting and reconnecting to the network:

    ○ Open **Settings** on your iPhone and go to **Wi-Fi**. Tap the **i** next to your connected network and choose **Forget This Network**.

    ○ After forgetting the network, reconnect by selecting the network and entering the password again.

3. This process can help resolve any connection issues between your Apple Watch and the Wi-Fi network.

4. **Check for Interference**
    Ensure that there are no physical barriers or electronic interference preventing your Apple Watch from connecting to Wi-Fi. Sometimes, interference from other devices can disrupt the connection.

5. **Reboot Your Router**
    If your Apple Watch continues to have Wi-Fi issues, try rebooting your Wi-Fi router. This can often help reset network settings and improve connectivity.

Fixing Bluetooth Connectivity Issues

Bluetooth connectivity is essential for pairing your Apple Watch with your iPhone and other devices, such as wireless headphones or fitness equipment. If you're having trouble connecting your Apple Watch via Bluetooth, here's how to fix it:

1. **Check Bluetooth Settings**

   o   Ensure that Bluetooth is turned on both on your Apple Watch and iPhone. On your iPhone, go to **Settings > Bluetooth**, and make sure that Bluetooth is toggled on.

   o   On your Apple Watch, swipe up on the watch face to open the **Control Center**, and make sure the **Bluetooth icon** is active.

2. **Reconnect Bluetooth Devices**
   If your Apple Watch isn't connecting to Bluetooth accessories (such as AirPods), try turning Bluetooth off and back on. On your iPhone, go to **Settings > Bluetooth**, and toggle Bluetooth off and on again. Similarly, you can turn Bluetooth off on your watch by going to **Settings > Bluetooth**.

3. **Unpair and Re-pair Your Devices**
   If your Apple Watch is not pairing with your iPhone via Bluetooth, try unpairing and repairing them:

   o   On your iPhone, open the **Apple Watch app**, select **My Watch**, and tap **Unpair Apple Watch**.

   o   After unpairing, set up the Apple Watch again and pair it with your iPhone.

4. **Reset Network Settings**
   If Bluetooth issues persist, try resetting your **network settings** on your iPhone. Go to **Settings > General > Reset > Reset Network Settings**. This will reset all Wi-Fi, cellular, and Bluetooth connections, and you will need to reconnect to your Wi-Fi and Bluetooth devices afterward.

Fixing iPhone Syncing Issues

Sometimes, your Apple Watch may not sync with your iPhone, preventing you from receiving notifications, messages, or other important updates. To fix iPhone syncing issues, follow these steps:

1. **Check Bluetooth and Wi-Fi**
   Ensure that both Bluetooth and Wi-Fi are turned on for both your iPhone and Apple Watch. This is essential for syncing data between the devices.

2. **Restart Both Devices**
   Restart both your **iPhone** and **Apple Watch** to refresh their connection. Restarting both devices can help resolve syncing issues that may arise from temporary glitches.

3. **Unpair and Re-pair Your Devices**
   If the syncing issue persists, try unpairing and repairing your Apple Watch with your iPhone:

   ○ Open the **Apple Watch app** on your iPhone and select **My Watch**.

   ○ Tap **Unpair Apple Watch**, then follow the instructions to unpair the watch.

   ○ After unpairing, pair your Apple Watch with your iPhone again and check if the syncing issue is resolved.

4. **Check for Software Updates**
   Ensure both your iPhone and Apple Watch are running the latest software updates. Go to **Settings > General > Software Update** on your iPhone and Apple Watch to check for available updates.

Solving Notification Problems

Notifications are one of the most significant aspects of the Apple Watch, alerting you to calls, texts, and app changes. However, there may be occasions when notifications aren't operating correctly, and this might lead to missed messages or vital alerts. Below are some steps to troubleshoot and address notification difficulties.

How to Fix Notification Issues

1. **Check Notification Settings**
   Make sure your notification settings are configured correctly:

   - On your iPhone, open the **Apple Watch app**, tap **My Watch**, and go to **Notifications**. Here, you can control how and when you receive notifications from different apps.

   - On your Apple Watch, swipe up to open the **Control Center**, and ensure that **Do Not Disturb** is turned off.

2. **Check Sound and Haptic Settings**
   If you aren't hearing or feeling notifications, check your sound and haptic settings. On your Apple Watch, go to **Settings > Sounds & Haptics** to ensure that both sound and haptic feedback are enabled. You can also increase the haptic strength to make notifications more noticeable.

3. **Reboot Your Apple Watch**
   If notifications are still not working, try restarting your Apple Watch to reset any glitches that may be affecting the system.

4. **Re-pair Apple Watch with iPhone**
   If the issue persists, consider unpairing and repairing your Apple Watch with your iPhone, as explained earlier. This often resolves syncing and notification issues.

While the Apple Watch Series 10 is designed to be user-friendly and reliable, issues do sometimes develop that require debugging. Whether it's restarting your device, correcting connectivity problems, or resolving notification issues, understanding how to troubleshoot your watch can save you time and stress.

Updating watchOS Without Hassle

Keeping your Apple Watch's software up to date is critical for ensuring it runs properly, performs efficiently, and remains secure. watchOS, the operating system that drives the Apple Watch, routinely receives upgrades to improve speed, repair issues, and add new capabilities. For seniors, the process of updating software can seem a bit daunting, but it is necessary for maintaining the device's operation.

Why Updating watchOS is Important

Updating your watchOS regularly is essential for several reasons:

- **Security**: Updates often include important security patches that protect your data and personal information.

- **Bug Fixes**: Updates resolve minor software bugs that could cause the watch to freeze, run slowly, or malfunction.

- **New Features**: Apple regularly introduces new features that can enhance the user experience, improve health tracking, and optimize app performance.

- **Compatibility**: If you use third-party apps or connect the watch with other devices, keeping the software up to date ensures compatibility and optimal performance.

How to Update watchOS

Updating watchOS on your Apple Watch is a simple process, but it's important to follow the correct steps to ensure everything goes smoothly. Here's how you can update your Apple Watch without hassle:

1. Check for Updates

Before you start the update process, check if there's a new version of watchOS available. To do this:

1. **Open the Apple Watch app** on your paired iPhone.

2. Tap **My Watch** at the bottom of the screen.

3. Scroll down and tap **General**, then tap **Software Update**.

4. If an update is available, you'll see the option to **Download and Install** it. If your watch is already up to date, the app will tell you that your watchOS is the latest version.

2. Prepare Your Devices for the Update

To avoid any interruptions during the update process, make sure both your **iPhone** and **Apple Watch** are properly prepared:

- **Charge Your Devices**: Make sure your **Apple Watch** has at least **50% battery** before starting the update. It's also a good idea to keep your **iPhone** charged and connected to a stable Wi-Fi network.

- **Connect to Wi-Fi**: Your **iPhone** should be connected to a **Wi-Fi network** to download the update. The update cannot be downloaded over cellular data, so make sure your Wi-Fi is stable.

3. Start the Update

Once your devices are prepared, you can begin the update process:

1. On your **iPhone**, tap **Download and Install** when you see the update prompt.

2. If asked, enter your **iPhone passcode**.

3. The update will then begin downloading. This process may take several minutes depending on the size of the update and the speed of your internet connection.

4. After the download is complete, the Apple Watch will automatically begin the installation process. Your watch will restart during the installation, and it will take some time to complete.

4. Wait for the Update to Finish

Once the update begins, let the process run to completion. Do not interrupt the process by turning off the devices or attempting to use them. Your Apple Watch will display a progress bar, and once the update is installed, it will automatically restart and be ready to use.

5. Verify the Update

After the update completes, verify that the new version of watchOS has been successfully installed by going back to **Settings > General > Software Update** on your Apple Watch. It should display the latest version number.

Common Update Problems and Fixes

While updating your Apple Watch is typically straightforward, there may be occasional issues that arise:

- **Update Stuck or Frozen**: If the update seems to be stuck, restart both your iPhone and Apple Watch. Then, try the update process again.

- **Update Failed**: If the update fails to install, try removing the watch from your iPhone and repairing it. You can also try updating via the **Apple Watch app** on your iPhone if direct updates through the watch are not working.

- **Not Enough Storage**: If your Apple Watch doesn't have enough storage to complete the update, try deleting unused apps or content from your watch to free up space.

Battery Tips: Extending Battery Life

The battery life of your Apple Watch Series 10 is one of its most significant aspects. A long-lasting battery guarantees that you can use your watch throughout the day for all its functionality, from tracking workouts to receiving texts. However, like any gadget, battery life might decline with time or may not last as long if settings and usage aren't optimal. Fortunately, there are various ways to maximize your Apple Watch's battery life.

Understanding Battery Life Expectations

The Apple Watch Series 10 is meant to give up to 18 hours of battery life on a single charge, with typical use. This includes checking the clock, utilizing apps, receiving messages, and tracking activities like exercise. However, certain functions and settings can cause the battery to deplete faster.

Tips to Extend Battery Life on Your Apple Watch

1. **Use Power Reserve Mode**
   Power Reserve mode is a helpful feature when your battery is running low and you need to conserve energy. When Power Reserve is activated, your Apple Watch will only display the time, and all other features (like apps and notifications) will be disabled.
   To activate **Power Reserve**, press and hold the **Side Button**, then swipe the slider to the **Power Reserve** position.

2. **Reduce Screen Brightness**
   A bright screen can drain your Apple Watch's battery quickly. To reduce brightness:

   ○ Open **Settings > Display & Brightness** on your Apple Watch.

   ○ Use the slider to adjust the brightness level. Lowering the brightness will help save battery without sacrificing usability.

3. **Disable Always-On Display**
   The **Always-On Display** feature, which shows the time and watch face even when your wrist is down, can be convenient, but it consumes more battery. If you prefer longer battery life:

o   Go to **Settings** > **Display & Brightness**, and toggle off **Always On**.

4. **Disable Unnecessary Notifications**
   Receiving frequent notifications can drain your battery. If you don't need notifications for certain apps, consider turning them off:

   o   Go to **Settings** > **Notifications** and customize which apps are allowed to send notifications. Disable notifications for apps you don't need immediate alerts for.

5. **Turn Off Background App Refresh**
   The **Background App Refresh** feature allows apps to update in the background, but it can consume more power. To turn off background updates:

   o   Open **Settings** > **General** > **Background App Refresh** and turn it off for apps you don't need updating in the background.

6. **Disable Unused Features (e.g., Wi-Fi, Bluetooth)**
   If you're not using **Wi-Fi**, **Bluetooth**, or **Cellular**, it's a good idea to turn them off to save battery:

   o   Swipe up on the watch face to open the **Control Center** and turn off these features when not in use.

7. **Use Low Power Mode**
   If your watch's battery is running low and you need to extend its life, **Low Power Mode** can help. This reduces power consumption by disabling certain features like automatic app refresh and background updates. To enable **Low Power Mode**, swipe up to access the **Control Center**, and tap the **Low Power Mode** icon (a yellow battery icon).

8. **Check Battery Health**
   Over time, the battery's maximum capacity will degrade. To check the health of your battery:

   o   Open **Settings** > **Battery** on your Apple Watch and tap **Battery Health**. This will show you the maximum capacity and performance capabilities of your watch's battery.

9. **Keep Software Updated**
   Apple regularly releases updates to improve performance and battery efficiency. Make

sure your Apple Watch is always running the latest version of watchOS to benefit from these optimizations.

Battery Charging Tips

To ensure your battery lasts longer in the long term, avoid extreme temperatures and do not let the battery consistently drain to 0% before charging. Charge your Apple Watch when it's at around 20-30% to help maintain battery health.

When to Contact Apple Support

Despite following the troubleshooting tips above, there may be situations where your Apple Watch still isn't performing as expected. In these cases, it's best to contact **Apple Support** for further assistance. Here are a few scenarios in which it's a good idea to reach out for professional help:

1. **Persistent Software Issues**
   If your Apple Watch is continually freezing, crashing, or not updating, and the usual troubleshooting methods (like restarting or resetting) haven't helped, there may be a more serious software issue that requires professional assistance.

2. **Battery Issues**
   If your battery is draining unusually fast despite optimizing settings or if the battery isn't charging properly, it may be a sign that the battery is damaged or defective. Apple Support can help determine whether a battery replacement is necessary.

3. **Hardware Problems**
   If your Apple Watch has sustained physical damage, such as a cracked screen, broken buttons, or issues with the sensors, it's best to contact Apple Support to see if the watch is eligible for repair or replacement.

4. **Unresponsive Features or Apps**
   If specific features (such as **Wi-Fi**, **Bluetooth**, or **Health Monitoring**) aren't working, and troubleshooting hasn't resolved the problem, Apple Support can help investigate the issue and recommend further steps.

5. **When You Can't Unpair or Reset the Watch**
   If you're unable to unpair your Apple Watch from your iPhone or perform a factory

reset, Apple Support can guide you through the process or assist in troubleshooting more advanced issues.

How to Contact Apple Support

1. **Apple Support App**
   The **Apple Support app** is a convenient way to get help directly on your iPhone. You can use the app to chat with a support representative, schedule an appointment at an Apple Store, or call for assistance.

2. **Apple's Website**
   Visit **support.apple.com** to find FAQs, troubleshooting guides, and more information about your Apple Watch. You can also use the website to schedule a call or chat with a support agent.

3. **Apple Store**
   If necessary, you can take your Apple Watch to an **Apple Store** for an in-person consultation. Genius Bar appointments are available for troubleshooting and repairs.

4. **AppleCare+**
   If you have **AppleCare+**, Apple's extended warranty and service plan, you can receive additional support and coverage for repairs, including battery replacements and accidental damage.

Troubleshooting and maintaining your Apple Watch Series 10 is a simple yet crucial component of keeping your device functioning properly. By following the instructions provided in this chapter, you may address common issues such as software updates, battery life, and connectivity problems with simplicity. Remember that your Apple Watch is designed to be straightforward, and by employing a few basic troubleshooting techniques, you can easily resolve most issues.

If the problem persists, don't hesitate to reach out to Apple Support for more specialized assistance. By understanding how to maintain and repair your Apple Watch, you'll guarantee it continues to be a beneficial companion for your daily life—whether you're using it to check your health, stay connected, or simply enjoy its capabilities.

Chapter 11

Tips, Tricks, and Hidden Features

The Apple Watch Series 10 is a fantastic device, filled with a wide range of functions meant to simplify and enhance daily living. However, many users—especially seniors—may not be aware of the tips, techniques, and hidden functions that can greatly enrich their experience with the watch. The Apple Watch includes various time-saving shortcuts, intuitive gestures, and quick methods to access your favorite tasks that can make using the watch even quicker and more efficient.

In this chapter, we'll unearth these useful insights and hidden features to guarantee you're getting the most out of your Apple Watch. Whether you're trying to save time, discover new motions, or quickly access critical functions, we'll take you through everything you need to know to make your Apple Watch experience as easy and pleasurable as possible.

Time-Saving Tips for Daily Use

One of the most attractive features of the Apple Watch is how it can streamline your daily tasks. The Apple Watch allows you to finish tasks, remain connected, and manage your schedule more efficiently. In this part, we'll explore numerous time-saving methods that will help you use your Apple Watch to its greatest potential.

Set Up Notifications Wisely

Notifications are one of the Apple Watch's distinguishing features, but managing them well may make a major difference in how fast and efficiently you use your watch. By customizing the notifications you receive and how they appear, you may keep informed without feeling overwhelmed.

How to Set Custom Notification Preferences

1. **Open the Apple Watch App on Your iPhone**
   Begin by opening the **Apple Watch app** on your iPhone. Tap **My Watch** at the bottom of the screen.

2. **Choose Notifications**

    Scroll down and tap on **Notifications**. Here, you can manage notifications from each app individually. You can decide which apps will show alerts on your watch and how those alerts will appear. For example, you can set some apps to send only a gentle tap and others to send a full notification.

3. **Set Notification Settings for Priority Apps**

    For apps that are most important to you (such as Messages or Calendar), set them to show notifications prominently, while silencing or disabling notifications for less critical apps. This ensures that you receive important information without unnecessary distractions.

4. **Using Do Not Disturb and Focus Modes**

    You can also use **Do Not Disturb** or **Focus Mode** to temporarily silence notifications when you need to concentrate or relax. Swipe up from the bottom of the watch face to access the **Control Center**, then tap the **crescent moon icon** to enable Do Not Disturb.

By customizing notifications, you'll be able to filter out the noise and focus only on what's important, saving you time and energy throughout the day.

Use Siri for Quick Tasks

Siri, Apple's voice assistant, is a fantastic tool for performing quick tasks without needing to manually interact with your watch. You can ask Siri to set reminders, send messages, check the weather, or perform other tasks hands-free.

How to Activate and Use Siri

1. **Activate Siri by Saying "Hey Siri"**

    Simply raise your wrist and say "Hey Siri" to activate the voice assistant without touching the watch. From here, you can ask Siri to perform a variety of tasks, such as "What's the weather today?" or "Set a reminder for 2 PM."

2. **Use the Side Button for Siri**

    Alternatively, you can press and hold the **Side Button** to activate Siri manually. This is useful if you prefer not to use voice activation.

3. **Create Reminders and Alarms**

    With Siri, you can create reminders and alarms on the go. For example, you can say, "Siri, remind me to take my medication at 4 PM," and Siri will set the reminder for you.

4. **Control Apps and Settings with Siri**
   Siri also lets you control settings like adjusting the volume, turning on or off Do Not Disturb mode, or playing music. "Hey Siri, play my workout playlist" is just one example of how you can quickly get things done with Siri.

Using Siri reduces the need for multiple taps, saving you time and effort.

Use the "Back to" Feature for Quick App Switching

Apple Watch's **Back to** feature allows you to quickly return to the previous app or action you were using without needing to go back to the Home Screen. This is a simple but powerful time-saver.

How to Use the "Back to" Feature

- **Swipe Right**: If you're in an app and want to return to the previous screen or app, simply swipe right. This will instantly take you back to where you were, eliminating the need to press the Digital Crown multiple times.

This small trick helps you move between tasks seamlessly without having to re-enter menus, keeping you on track and saving time.

Customize Your Watch Face for Quick Access to Apps

Your watch face is more than just a place to check the time—it's a useful area for displaying information and quick access to apps you use most often. By customizing your watch face, you can save time and avoid searching through the app list.

How to Customize Your Watch Face

1. **Choose a Watch Face**
   Press and hold your current watch face to access the customization screen. Swipe through the available watch faces and tap the one you want to customize.

2. **Add Complications**
   Complications are small widgets that display information directly on the watch face, such as your heart rate, the weather, or upcoming calendar events. Tap on a complication to change what it displays, and add the ones that matter most to you.

3. **Set Up Shortcuts on Your Watch Face**
   Many watch faces allow you to add quick-access shortcuts to your most-used apps, such as the Workout app, Contacts, or Messages. By adding these shortcuts to your watch face, you can access them instantly with a single tap.

Customizing your watch face saves you time and helps you stay organized, putting the most important information right at your fingertips.

Hidden Gestures You Should Know

The Apple Watch Series 10 is filled with handy gestures that can make interacting with your watch faster and more intuitive. Many of these gestures are buried in plain sight, and knowing how to utilize them might help you get more out of your device without needing to tap through multiple screens.

Quickly Access the Control Center

The **Control Center** gives you access to essential settings, such as Do Not Disturb, battery life, Wi-Fi, and more. Instead of digging through menus, you can access the **Control Center** with a simple swipe.

How to Access the Control Center

- **Swipe Down from the Top of the Watch Face**: To access the Control Center, swipe down from the top edge of the Apple Watch screen. This gives you quick access to settings like **battery life**, **Do Not Disturb**, **Airplane mode**, and more.

- **Swipe Up to Close**: To close the Control Center, simply swipe up on the screen again.

Switch Between Apps with the App Switcher

Apple Watch Series 10 allows you to quickly switch between apps using the **App Switcher**. This is especially useful if you're frequently switching between apps or need to close apps that are running in the background.

How to Use the App Switcher

1. **Press the Side Button Twice**: Quickly double-press the **Side Button** to bring up the **App Switcher**. This will show you a carousel of recently used apps.

2. **Scroll Through Apps**: Swipe left or right to scroll through the apps you've used recently. Tap an app to open it directly, or swipe it up to close it.

Zoom In and Out on the Watch Face

Sometimes, the text on your Apple Watch can be hard to read, especially if you have vision impairments. Fortunately, Apple Watch allows you to zoom in and out to make reading easier.

How to Zoom

- **Enable Zoom**: Go to **Settings** > **Accessibility** > **Zoom**, then turn on **Zoom**.

- **Zoom In or Out**: Once enabled, double-tap the screen with two fingers to zoom in or out. You can also drag your fingers to move around the screen and view the content more clearly.

Use the Digital Crown for Scrolling

The **Digital Crown** on the side of your Apple Watch isn't just for waking up the watch or changing the time. It's also a convenient tool for scrolling through apps, messages, and notifications without touching the screen.

How to Use the Digital Crown for Scrolling

1. **Scroll**: To scroll through a list or read a long message, simply rotate the **Digital Crown**. This allows you to move through content without having to swipe or tap.

2. **Zoom**: You can also use the **Digital Crown** to zoom in on text or images, making it easier to read and view details on the screen.

Use Force Touch for Extra Options

Although newer models of the Apple Watch have moved away from Force Touch, the **Apple Watch Series 10** still has a pressure-sensitive touch feature that can give you extra options when interacting with apps.

How to Use Force Touch

1. **Press Firmly on the Screen**: To bring up additional options, press firmly on the screen when using certain apps or features. For example, pressing firmly on the watch face lets you quickly switch faces, while Force Touch in the Messages app allows you to delete conversations.

Quick Access to Favorite Features

Apple Watch Series 10 allows you to set up quick shortcuts to your favorite features, making them easily accessible without needing to scroll through menus. These features save you time and give you faster access to the things you use the most.

Add Shortcuts to Your Watch Face

As mentioned earlier, you can add **complications** to your watch face to display important information or provide quick access to apps. However, you can also add **shortcuts** to favorite apps for even faster access.

How to Add Shortcuts

1. **Customize Your Watch Face**: Press and hold your current watch face to bring up the customization screen.

2. **Select Shortcuts**: Choose from a variety of app shortcuts, such as **Phone**, **Messages**, or **Health**, and place them on your watch face.

3. **Tap to Access**: With these shortcuts added, you can access your favorite apps with just a tap.

Use Siri Shortcuts for Fast Access

If you use certain apps or actions frequently, Siri Shortcuts is a great way to automate these tasks. Siri Shortcuts allows you to create custom voice commands to launch apps, set reminders, or trigger actions.

How to Create Siri Shortcuts

1. **Open the Shortcuts App**: On your iPhone, open the **Shortcuts app**.

2. **Create a New Shortcut**: Tap the + icon to create a new shortcut. Choose the action you want Siri to perform, such as opening an app or sending a message.

3. **Add to Watch**: Once your shortcut is created, you can add it to your Apple Watch for quick access.

The Apple Watch Series 10 is packed with hidden features, time-saving recommendations, and simple shortcuts that can make your daily tasks faster and more effective. From leveraging Siri for quick chores to understanding secret gestures and creating shortcuts for your favorite apps, these hacks are designed to help you get the most out of your iPhone. By adopting these recommendations, you can unleash the full potential of your Apple Watch and enjoy a better, more intuitive user experience.

Voice Commands Seniors Will Love

Apple Watch Series 10 incorporates Siri, Apple's speech assistant, which can make your life much easier by allowing you to execute tasks with nothing but your voice. This hands-free interaction can be immensely advantageous for elders, making it easier to access information and execute chores without needing to tap on the screen.

What Siri Can Do for You

Siri is capable of accomplishing a broad number of tasks on your Apple Watch. From setting reminders and sending texts to delivering information and controlling your smart home devices, Siri can aid you with many facets of your everyday routine. Below are some of the most useful voice commands for seniors:

1. Setting Reminders and Alarms

Forgetfulness is something that can affect us all, but with Siri, it's easier than ever to stay organized and remember important tasks. You can ask Siri to remind you to take medication, attend appointments, or complete any daily tasks.

- **Command Example**: "Hey Siri, remind me to take my medication at 3 PM."

- **Command Example**: "Hey Siri, set an alarm for 7 AM tomorrow."

Siri will create a reminder or alarm for you, making sure that you don't forget important activities throughout the day.

2. Sending Texts and Messages

Sometimes typing on the small screen can be difficult, but Siri makes it easy to send messages with just your voice. Whether you want to send a quick text to a loved one or respond to an incoming message, Siri can help.

- **Command Example**: "Hey Siri, send a text to John saying I'm running late."

- **Command Example**: "Hey Siri, reply to this message with 'Thank you!'"

You can also use **dictation** to reply to messages or emails, making it a quick and efficient way to communicate with others, especially when you're on the go.

3. Getting Directions and Information

Whether you're heading to a new location or just want to know the weather, Siri is your go-to assistant. By simply asking, you can receive real-time updates on directions, weather forecasts, and more.

- **Command Example**: "Hey Siri, give me directions to the nearest pharmacy."

- **Command Example**: "Hey Siri, what's the weather like today?"

- **Command Example**: "Hey Siri, how far is the nearest grocery store?"

By using Siri to get directions, you can avoid having to manually type addresses or look things up on your phone.

4. Controlling Smart Home Devices

If you have **smart home devices**, Siri can control them for you directly from your Apple Watch. You can turn on lights, adjust the thermostat, lock doors, and more—all without leaving the comfort of your wrist.

- **Command Example**: "Hey Siri, turn off the living room lights."

- **Command Example**: "Hey Siri, set the thermostat to 70 degrees."

This is particularly helpful for seniors who may have mobility challenges or simply want to control their environment with minimal effort.

5. Making Calls and Setting up Voicemail

Making calls is easy with Siri. Whether you're calling a family member, friend, or a healthcare provider, Siri can make the process hands-free.

- **Command Example**: "Hey Siri, call Mary."

- **Command Example**: "Hey Siri, set up voicemail."

This voice command eliminates the need to scroll through contacts, letting you make calls quickly and without hassle.

Managing Multiple Watch Faces for Different Needs

Apple Watch Series 10 offers the opportunity to customize your watch face, and one of the most significant features is the ability to have various watch faces for different requirements and scenarios. This capability might help you tailor your watch for certain activities, moods, or tasks. For elderly, having numerous watch faces might improve accessibility and convenience.

Why Multiple Watch Faces Are Useful for Seniors

Having several different watch faces allows you to quickly switch between different modes, depending on your needs. For example:

- **Health and Fitness**: Use a watch face that displays **heart rate**, **step count**, and **activity rings** when you're exercising or focused on staying active.

- **Social and Communication**: Choose a watch face with **notifications** and **messages** prominently displayed when you need to stay connected with loved ones.

- **Travel or Navigation**: Set a watch face with **maps** or **directions** if you're going somewhere and need to keep track of your route.

- **Simple and Minimalist**: Select a watch face with just the time and date for days when you don't need any distractions.

How to Manage and Switch Between Watch Faces

1. **Add New Watch Faces**
   To add a new watch face, press and hold your current watch face, then swipe left or right to see available watch face options. If you want to add more faces, tap the + icon at the end of the screen.

2. **Customize Your Watch Faces**
   Once you've selected a face, you can customize it by tapping **Customize**. Here, you can adjust features like:

   - **Complications**: Add small widgets that show information like your calendar, activity rings, heart rate, and more.

   - **Color and Style**: Change the color and design of the watch face to suit your preferences.

    ○ **Functionality**: Depending on the watch face, you can customize the layout and the specific information it displays.

3. **Switch Between Watch Faces**

    To switch between watch faces, press and hold your current watch face, then swipe left or right to select a different face. You can also create **shortcuts** or **complications** on your watch face for quick access to apps or information.

4. **Set a Watch Face for Specific Activities**

    By customizing your watch faces to match your lifestyle, you can easily have the information you need right at your fingertips. For example, when exercising, you can have a face that focuses on fitness data. When heading out, have a face that shows your next appointments and maps.

5. **Use the "Back to" Feature**

    Apple Watch also offers a handy feature called **Back to** that lets you quickly return to the previous screen or app you were using. It's a simple but effective way to jump between apps or settings without unnecessary steps.

Advanced Features Simplified for Seniors

While the Apple Watch Series 10 offers many advanced functions, it's vital to remember that not all of them need to be complex. This section will simplify some of the more complicated capabilities so that you may utilize them confidently without feeling overwhelmed.

Using Health and Fitness Features for Seniors

Apple Watch is well-known for its health and fitness tracking capabilities, and these features are especially important for seniors who wish to keep active and healthy. Some advanced features can make a major difference in your wellness routine without requiring complicated settings.

1. Heart Rate Monitoring

The Apple Watch continuously tracks your heart rate, providing you with vital information about your cardiovascular health. For seniors, monitoring heart rate can be crucial, especially for those with existing health conditions.

- **How to Use**: Open the **Heart Rate app** on your Apple Watch to view your current heart rate. You can also monitor your heart rate continuously through the **Health app** on your iPhone.

2. Fall Detection

If you've experienced a fall, the Apple Watch can automatically detect it and alert emergency services. It's a critical feature for seniors, offering peace of mind in case of an accident.

- **How to Enable**: Go to **Settings > Emergency SOS** on your Apple Watch, then toggle on **Fall Detection**.

3. ECG and Blood Oxygen Monitoring

The Apple Watch Series 10 can measure your **ECG (electrocardiogram)** and **blood oxygen levels**, which can be important for seniors who are managing chronic health conditions or simply want to track their overall well-being.

- **How to Use**: Open the **ECG app** to take an ECG reading, and use the **Blood Oxygen app** to check your oxygen levels.

Making Use of Siri for Advanced Features

Siri is an advanced voice assistant that can handle many complex tasks with ease. By speaking to Siri, seniors can perform advanced functions without ever needing to interact directly with the watch.

Control Smart Devices

- **Command Example**: "Hey Siri, dim the living room lights."

- This can control smart home devices like thermostats, lights, and security systems, all from your wrist.

Activate and Control Apps

- **Command Example**: "Hey Siri, open the Maps app and get directions to the nearest hospital."

- Siri can launch apps, set reminders, and even interact with apps, saving you time and effort.

Simplifying Apple Pay for Seniors

Apple Pay allows you to make secure payments directly from your Apple Watch. While it's an advanced feature, using it is easy once set up.

1. **Set Up Apple Pay**: Open the **Wallet app** on your iPhone, add your credit or debit cards, and enable Apple Pay.

2. **Make Payments**: Simply double-press the **Side Button** on your Apple Watch and hold it near a contactless payment terminal to complete your transaction.

This feature eliminates the need for carrying cash or credit cards, making payments faster and more secure.

The Apple Watch Series 10 is a powerful gadget that offers a wide range of capabilities designed to simplify your life, especially with the tips, tricks, and hidden features we've explored in this chapter. Whether you're using voice commands, maintaining various watch faces for different activities, or employing advanced capabilities like ECG and Apple Pay, your watch can be a genuinely personal assistant.

By using these recommendations and understanding the watch's capabilities, you can make the most out of your Apple Watch, adapting it to your individual needs and lifestyle. In the following chapter, we will go further into more personalized settings and options to ensure that your Apple Watch continues to enhance your life in a meaningful way.

Chapter 12

Beyond the Basics: Mastering Your Watch

The Apple Watch Series 10 is far more than simply a fitness tracker or a quick way to check the time. It's a comprehensive device that connects smoothly with other Apple products, giving a unique experience that enhances your life by linking all of your Apple devices. For seniors, this means that not only can you stay in touch with family and friends and track your health, but you can also control several devices from the ease of your wrist.

In this chapter, we will explore the full potential of your Apple Watch, going beyond the fundamentals. We'll discuss how to connect your Apple Watch with other Apple devices, such as your iPad, Mac, and Apple TV, and how to control your smart home gadgets with HomeKit. With these capabilities, you can expand the usability of your Apple Watch and make it even more valuable as an integrated part of your Apple ecosystem.

Using the Apple Watch with Other Apple Devices

One of the best features of owning many Apple devices is the seamless connection between them. The Apple Watch Series 10 works flawlessly with your iPhone, iPad, Mac, and Apple TV. This interoperability allows you to move between devices with ease, access content across platforms, and control all parts of your Apple environment from your wrist.

How Apple Watch Syncs with iPhone

The Apple Watch is designed to function primarily with your iPhone, and syncing between the two is simple and uncomplicated. The Apple Watch relies on your iPhone for many of its essential operations, such as getting notifications, sending messages, and syncing apps.

Syncing Basics

1. **Pairing Apple Watch with iPhone**

   ○ The initial setup process involves pairing your Apple Watch with your iPhone. Once paired, the two devices communicate wirelessly to sync information, including contacts, calendars, and settings.

- To pair, simply open the **Apple Watch app** on your iPhone, and follow the on-screen instructions. Make sure Bluetooth and Wi-Fi are enabled on your iPhone to ensure a smooth connection.

2. **Syncing Apps and Content**

- **Apps**: Once paired, apps from your iPhone can sync with your Apple Watch. If an app is compatible with watchOS, it will automatically install on your Apple Watch. You can also manually select which apps to install from the **Apple Watch app** on your iPhone.

- **Music, Podcasts, and Photos**: You can sync **music**, **podcasts**, and **photos** to your Apple Watch, making it easy to access your favorite content even when you don't have your iPhone with you. For instance, by syncing a playlist to your Apple Watch, you can enjoy music while exercising or walking without carrying your phone.

Managing Notifications

Once synchronized, your Apple Watch mimics the alerts from your iPhone. For seniors who may not always hear or notice their phone's notifications, the Apple Watch offers a more handy and accessible method to stay on top of messages, calls, reminders, and calendar events. You may select which notifications to get from the Apple Watch app on your iPhone.

Syncing with iPad, Mac, and Apple TV

While the Apple Watch's primary function is related to your iPhone, it also enables connection with other Apple products, like the iPad, Mac, and Apple TV. Here's how you can utilize your Apple Watch with these devices:

Syncing with iPad

Although the Apple Watch doesn't directly sync with the iPad in the same way it syncs with your iPhone, certain apps and features are accessible across both devices:

1. **iCloud Syncing**: When you use **iCloud** with your Apple Watch, you can access content like contacts, calendar events, and reminders on both your iPad and Apple Watch. For instance, any calendar event created on your iPad will automatically appear on your Apple Watch.

2. **Handoff**: The **Handoff** feature allows you to start a task on one Apple device and pick it up on another. For example, if you're reading an email on your iPad, you can continue

reading it on your Apple Watch, and vice versa. Handoff works with a variety of apps, including **Mail**, **Messages**, and **Safari**.

Syncing with Mac

Your Apple Watch can be used to unlock your **Mac** and interact with apps in various ways:

1. **Unlocking Your Mac**: One of the most useful features for seniors is the ability to unlock your Mac with your Apple Watch. Simply wear your Apple Watch, and when you wake your Mac, it will automatically detect the watch and unlock your computer. This feature eliminates the need to type in a password each time you access your Mac.

2. **Apple Pay on Mac**: If you make purchases online using **Apple Pay**, your Apple Watch can be used to authenticate the payment, eliminating the need to enter payment details manually. Simply confirm the payment using your watch.

Syncing with Apple TV

Your Apple Watch can also be used to control your **Apple TV**:

1. **Control Apple TV with Apple Watch**: While watching your favorite shows on **Apple TV**, you can use your Apple Watch to control volume, pause, or change channels with just a tap. This is a convenient feature for seniors who may have difficulty using the regular remote.

2. **AirPlay**: If you want to stream content from your Apple Watch to your **Apple TV**, you can use the **AirPlay** feature. For example, you can stream music, photos, or even workout data to your TV for a larger display.

Using HomeKit and Smart Devices from Your Watch

One of the striking features of the Apple Watch Series 10 is its ability to control smart home devices. With HomeKit, Apple's framework for controlling smart devices, your watch becomes a powerful tool for managing everything from lights and thermostats to locks and cameras, all with a simple tap or voice command.

What is HomeKit?

HomeKit is Apple's smart home framework that connects numerous smart devices, such as thermostats, lighting, locks, security cameras, and more. With HomeKit, you can control these gadgets from your iPhone, iPad, Mac, or Apple Watch. The integration between HomeKit and the Apple Watch allows you to manage your home's devices straight from your wrist, making it easier than ever to stay in charge of your environment.

Setting Up HomeKit on Your Apple Watch

To use **HomeKit** with your Apple Watch, you first need to set up your smart home devices and connect them to the **Home app** on your iPhone. Once everything is connected, you can control your smart devices directly from your Apple Watch.

1. **Set Up the Home App on iPhone**

   ○ Open the **Home app** on your iPhone and tap + to add new devices. Follow the instructions to connect each device to **HomeKit**.

   ○ If you have a **smart hub** (such as an Apple TV or iPad), ensure it's set up to control devices remotely when you're not at home.

2. **Use the Home App on Apple Watch**

   ○ Open the **Home app** on your Apple Watch by pressing the **Digital Crown** to go to the Home Screen and tapping the **Home app icon**.

   ○ The Home app on your Apple Watch shows you a summary of all connected devices. Tap any device to control it, such as turning off the lights, adjusting the thermostat, or checking the status of security cameras.

Controlling Smart Devices with Siri

If you have multiple smart devices in your home, controlling them with **Siri** on your Apple Watch is even faster and more efficient. Instead of scrolling through the Home app, you can simply use voice commands to control your smart home with ease.

How to Control Smart Devices with Siri

1. **Turn Off the Lights**: "Hey Siri, turn off the living room lights."

2. **Adjust the Thermostat**: "Hey Siri, set the thermostat to 72 degrees."

3. **Lock the Doors**: "Hey Siri, lock the front door."

4. **Check Security Cameras**: "Hey Siri, show me the front door camera."

With **Siri**, controlling your smart home is as easy as asking a question, allowing seniors to manage their home effortlessly from their wrist.

Setting Up Scenes and Automation

Scenes and **automation** allow you to control multiple devices at once or set up actions based on certain triggers. For example, you can create a **"Good Morning" scene that turns on your lights, adjusts the thermostat, and opens the blinds.**

How to Create Scenes and Automation

1. **Create a Scene**: In the **Home app** on your iPhone, tap + and select **Add Scene**. From here, you can add multiple devices to control at once.

2. **Set Automation**: You can create **automations** to trigger certain actions based on time of day, location, or even when a device is activated. For example, set your lights to automatically turn off when you leave the house or have your thermostat adjust when you arrive home.

Once your scenes and automation are set up, you can activate them directly from your Apple Watch with a single tap or voice command, making it even easier to manage your home environment.

The Apple Watch Series 10 is more than just a fitness tracker—it's a hub for managing and controlling your Apple ecosystem. By learning how to sync your Apple Watch with other Apple devices, control smart home devices with HomeKit, and use advanced capabilities across your iPhone, iPad, Mac, and Apple TV, you can unlock the full potential of your device and create a seamless, integrated experience.

Travel-Friendly Features: Time Zones, Currency, Language

Whether you're going across the nation or embarking on a global vacation, the Apple Watch Series 10 includes various travel-friendly features that make it the perfect companion for seniors on the go. These features are designed to make navigating new destinations, handling currency transactions, and communicating in other languages easier.

Managing Time Zones with Apple Watch

One of the most essential travel features on the Apple Watch Series 10 is its ability to manage time zones simply. Whether you're flying to a new city or simply traveling across time zones, your Apple Watch can automatically adjust and keep you on schedule.

How to Set Time Zones on Your Apple Watch

The Apple Watch automatically adjusts its time based on the time zone settings on your iPhone. When you travel to a new location, your watch will automatically adjust to the local time. However, there are a few parameters you need be aware of to guarantee this works correctly:

1. **Ensure Your iPhone Time Zone Settings Are Correct**
   The Apple Watch pulls its time from the **iPhone's time zone settings**. Make sure that your iPhone is set to **Automatic Time Zone** by going to **Settings > General > Date & Time**. Toggle on **Set Automatically**, and your Apple Watch will follow suit.

2. **Manually Change the Time Zone (If Needed)**
   In rare cases, you may need to manually adjust the time zone on your Apple Watch. To do this:

   - Open the **Clock app** on your Apple Watch.

   - Tap on the world clock, and then use the **search** feature to find your current location or desired city. This will display the time for that location alongside your own time zone.

3. **World Clock on Apple Watch**
   The **World Clock** complication on your watch face can be a convenient way to keep track of multiple time zones when traveling. Simply add the **World Clock** complication to your watch face, and you can easily see the time in different cities around the world.

Why Time Zone Features are Essential for Seniors

For seniors traveling internationally or between time zones, the ability to quickly adjust time settings ensures that you never miss an important event, such as a doctor's appointment or a meeting with family. By using the **World Clock** and the automatic time zone settings, you can stay organized and manage your schedule with ease while abroad.

Currency Conversion and Apple Watch

Another invaluable feature for seniors traveling abroad is the ability to easily convert currencies. Apple Watch's integration with **Siri** and third-party apps makes it possible to quickly calculate currency exchanges, so you're never caught off guard by foreign exchange rates.

Using Siri for Currency Conversion

With Siri on your Apple Watch, converting currency is as simple as asking a question. For example:

- **Command Example**: "Hey Siri, how much is 50 US dollars in euros?"

- **Command Example**: "Hey Siri, what's the exchange rate for British pounds to yen?"

Siri will provide an up-to-date exchange rate, saving you the time and hassle of looking up the rates manually. This is especially helpful when you need quick, on-the-spot information.

Using Currency Conversion Apps

In addition to Siri, several third-party apps are available on the **App Store** that can help you manage currency conversion. Apps like **XE Currency**, **Easy Currency Converter**, and others allow you to track multiple currencies in real-time. You can install these apps on your Apple Watch and access them directly from your wrist, ensuring you always have the latest rates available.

Language Translation for Travel

Language barriers are a common challenge when traveling to non-English-speaking countries. Fortunately, the Apple Watch Series 10 can assist in overcoming language barriers through its integration with **Siri** and translation apps.

Using Siri for Language Translation

With Siri, you can quickly translate phrases and sentences without needing a separate app. Simply ask Siri to translate for you, and she will provide an accurate translation. For example:

- **Command Example**: "Hey Siri, how do I say 'Where is the nearest hospital?' in French?"

- **Command Example**: "Hey Siri, translate 'I need help' into Spanish."

Using Translation Apps

While Siri can handle simple translations, for more intricate needs, you may wish to download a translation app that gives more extensive skills. Popular apps like Google Translate and iTranslate can be installed on your Apple Watch, allowing you to carry a whole dictionary and translation tool right on your wrist. These apps work offline, guaranteeing that you can always access them, even without a cellular connection or Wi-Fi.

Backing Up and Restoring Your Watch Data

Your Apple Watch holds a plethora of information, from health statistics and contacts to settings and preferences. It's vital to back up your watch regularly to avoid losing valuable data in the event of a problem or if you need to replace or reset the device.

How to Back Up Your Apple Watch

When you pair your Apple Watch with your iPhone, the watch's data is automatically backed up to **iCloud**. This makes restoring your watch's data easy if you ever need to reset it or set up a new watch.

Backing Up to iCloud

1. **Ensure iCloud Backup Is Enabled on iPhone**
   On your iPhone, open **Settings > [Your Name] > iCloud**, and make sure that **iCloud Backup** is turned on. This ensures that your Apple Watch data, including app settings, health information, and more, is backed up to the cloud.

2. **Automatic Backup During Pairing**
   Whenever your Apple Watch syncs with your iPhone, the data is automatically backed up. For instance, when you pair your watch with a new iPhone, all your apps, contacts, and settings will be transferred to the new device.

Manual Backups for Peace of Mind

Although Apple's automatic backup process is seamless, you can manually back up your Apple Watch data by unpairing it from your iPhone:

- Open the **Apple Watch app** on your iPhone.

- Tap **My Watch**, then select **Unpair Apple Watch**.

- The app will automatically create a backup of your Apple Watch's data before it unpairs.

This backup ensures that if you ever need to reset or replace your watch, you won't lose your important data.

How to Restore Your Watch Data

If you need to restore your Apple Watch data after a reset or when pairing a new watch, follow these steps:

1. **Unpair and Set Up Your Apple Watch**
   To begin the restore process, unpair your Apple Watch from your iPhone by opening the **Apple Watch app** and selecting **Unpair Apple Watch**.

2. **Restore from iCloud Backup**
   Once your watch is unpaired, follow the on-screen instructions to pair your Apple Watch with your iPhone again. During the setup process, you will be prompted to restore your watch from an **iCloud backup**. Select the most recent backup to restore all your data, including apps, settings, and health information.

Keeping Your Watch in Top Condition

Maintaining your Apple Watch Series 10 in good shape is vital for ensuring it lasts for years to come. From physical care to software maintenance, maintaining your watch in good form helps guarantee that it continues to function smoothly and efficiently.

Physical Care of Your Apple Watch

Apple Watches are built to last, but like any device, they can become worn over time if not taken care of properly. Here are some recommendations for keeping your watch in top condition:

1. Keep It Clean

Regular cleaning can help maintain the appearance of your Apple Watch. The **case**, **screen**, and **band** should be cleaned regularly to prevent dirt, dust, and bacteria buildup.

- Use a **soft, lint-free cloth** to clean the surface of the watch.

- If needed, lightly dampen the cloth with water (avoid using any cleaning agents or chemicals).

- Clean the watch's **bands** according to the material:

  - **Leather bands**: Wipe with a dry cloth. Avoid excessive moisture.

  - **Silicone bands**: These can be cleaned with mild soap and water.

  - **Metal bands**: Use a microfiber cloth to avoid scratching the surface.

2. Protect the Screen

If you want to prevent scratches and maintain the screen's clarity, consider applying a **screen protector**. This thin layer of protection can shield the display from everyday wear and tear.

3. Avoid Extreme Conditions

While the Apple Watch Series 10 is water-resistant, it's still important to avoid exposing it to extreme conditions. Avoid wearing your watch while swimming in hot tubs, using it in hot saunas, or exposing it to extreme humidity or temperatures for prolonged periods.

Maintaining Your Apple Watch's Battery Health

Proper battery maintenance ensures that your Apple Watch performs at its best over time. Here are some tips to help you maintain good battery health:

1. **Avoid Extreme Battery Drains**
   Try to keep your Apple Watch charged between **20% and 80%** for optimal battery health. Letting the battery completely drain or charging it to 100% frequently may reduce its lifespan.

2. **Use Low Power Mode When Needed**
   When you're running low on battery, use **Low Power Mode** to extend battery life. This reduces power consumption by disabling certain features like automatic app updates.

3. **Turn Off Unnecessary Features**
   Features like **Always-On Display**, **Bluetooth**, and **Wi-Fi** can drain the battery when left on. Turn off these features when you don't need them to conserve battery power.

Mastering your Apple Watch Series 10 is all about understanding its capabilities and using them to make your life easier.

From travel-friendly features that help you handle time zones, currencies, and language to backing up your data and maintaining your device in peak shape, your Apple Watch is designed to be a versatile and helpful tool for everyday life.

By learning how to sync your watch with other Apple devices, use sophisticated travel capabilities, and maintain your watch's functionality, you can guarantee that it remains a vital and trustworthy companion for years to come.

Whether you're traveling the world, keeping your data secure, or simply looking after your device, the Apple Watch Series 10 will always be ready to support your needs.

Conclusion

As we reach the final page of this book, remember this: the Apple Watch Series 10 is more than just a piece of technology—it's a gateway to a more connected, healthier, and empowered existence. Throughout this book, we've explored every part of your Apple Watch, from its basic capabilities to its hidden gems, from customizing your watch face to mastering voice commands, and from optimizing your health to staying seamlessly connected. Each chapter has equipped you with the tools and expertise to unlock the full potential of your smartphone, ensuring it serves you as an invaluable ally in your day-to-day life.

For elders, embracing technology may be revolutionary. The Apple Watch Series 10 allows you to stay active, check your health, and keep in touch with loved ones—all while allowing you to take responsibility for your well-being and daily activities. Whether you're tracking your fitness, managing your calendar, or exploring the world through the smart capabilities of your watch, the possibilities are unlimited. Technology no longer has to be daunting; with the appropriate advice and the correct tools, it provides a means to live smarter, healthier, and more independently.

The watch's ability to effortlessly interface with your iPhone, iPad, Mac, and Apple TV converts your Apple environment into a unified system of convenience. It's a continuous companion, whether you're at home or touring the world, delivering solutions to help you handle time zones, currencies, languages, and smart devices with ease.

As you continue forward on your adventure with the Apple Watch, remember that mastering technology is not about perfection—it's about progress. By taking tiny steps, trying with new features, and leaning into the support surrounding you, you'll grow more confident with every engagement. Your Apple Watch is a tool to better your life, but the actual power comes from your willingness to accept it, discover its functions, and make it your own.

keep confident, keep interested, and continue utilizing the Apple Watch Series 10 to enhance your life. It's more than just about remaining connected—it's about staying in control. Whether it's preserving your health, getting in touch with family, managing your daily activities, or simply enjoying the peace of mind that comes with knowing your device has your back, the Apple Watch Series 10 is here to support your journey every step of the way.

Thank you for taking the time to read this information. As you begin your adventure with your Apple Watch Series 10, know that you're not just mastering a technology; you're opening a new chapter in your life, full with opportunities, enhanced health, and connection. Embrace the technology, and let it enable you to live better, smarter, and more independently.